INTRODUCING
ISSUES WITH
OPPOSING
VIEWPOINTS®

Drug Abuse

Other books in the Introducing Issues
with Opposing Viewpoints series:

**INTRODUCING
ISSUES WITH
OPPOSING
VIEWPOINTS®**

Drug Abuse

Jacqueline Langwith, *Book Editor*

Christine Nasso, *Publisher*
Elizabeth Des Chenes, *Managing Editor*

GREENHAVEN PRESS
An imprint of Thomson Gale, a part of The Thomson Corporation

THOMSON
™
GALE

Detroit • New York • San Francisco • New Haven, Conn. • Waterville, Maine • London

LIBRARY OF CONGRESS CATALOGING-IN-PUBLICATION DATA

Drug abuse / Jacqueline Langwith, book editor.
    p. cm. — (Introducing issues with opposing viewpoints)
  Includes bibliographical references and index.
ISBN-13: 978-0-7377-3566-6 (hardcover : alk. paper)
ISBN-10: 0-7377-3566-X (hardcover : alk. paper)
  1. Drug abuse—United States. 2. Youth—Drug use—United States. I. Langwith, Jacqueline.
  HV5825.D75 2007
  362.290973—dc2

                    2006029460

Contents

Chapter 3: What Role Does Marijuana Play in Drug Abuse?

Foreword

I ndulging in a wide spectrum of ideas, beliefs, and perspectives is a critical cornerstone of democracy. After all, it is often debates over differences of opinion, such as whether to legalize abortion, how to treat prisoners, or when to enact the death penalty, that shape our society and drive it forward. Such diversity of thought is frequently regarded as the hallmark of a healthy and civilized culture. As the Reverend Clifford Schutjer of the First Congregational Church in Mansfield, Ohio, declared in a 2001 sermon, "Surrounding oneself with only like-minded people, restricting what we listen to or read only to what we find agreeable is irresponsible. Refusing to entertain doubts once we make up our minds is a subtle but deadly form of arrogance." With this advice in mind, Introducing Issues with Opposing Viewpoints books aim to open readers' minds to the critically divergent views that comprise our world's most important debates.

Introducing Issues with Opposing Viewpoints simplifies for students the enormous and often overwhelming mass of material now available via print and electronic media. Collected in every volume is an array of opinions that captures the essence of a particular controversy or topic. Introducing Issues with Opposing Viewpoints books embody the spirit of nineteenth-century journalist Charles A. Dana's axiom: "Fight for your opinions, but do not believe that they contain the whole truth, or the only truth." Absorbing such contrasting opinions teaches students to analyze the strength of an argument and compare it to its opposition. From this process readers can inform and strengthen their own opinions, or be exposed to new information that will change their minds. Introducing Issues with Opposing Viewpoints is a mosaic of different voices. The authors are statesmen, pundits, academics, journalists, corporations, and ordinary people who have felt compelled to share their experiences and ideas in a public forum. Their words have been collected from newspapers, journals, books, speeches, interviews, and the Internet, the fastest growing body of opinionated material in the world.

Introducing Issues with Opposing Viewpoints shares many of the well-known features of its critically acclaimed parent series, Opposing Viewpoints. The articles are presented in a pro/con format, allowing readers to absorb divergent perspectives side by side. Active reading questions preface each viewpoint, requiring the student to approach the material thoughtfully and carefully. Useful charts, graphs, and cartoons supplement each article. A thorough introduction provides readers with crucial background on an issue. An annotated bibliography points the reader toward articles, books, and Web sites that contain additional information on the topic. An appendix of organizations to contact contains a wide variety of charities, nonprofit organizations, political groups, and private enterprises that each hold a position on the issue at hand. Finally, a comprehensive index allows readers to locate content quickly and efficiently.

Introducing Issues with Opposing Viewpoints is also significantly different from Opposing Viewpoints. As the series title implies, its presentation will help introduce students to the concept of opposing viewpoints, and learn to use this material to aid in critical writing and debate. The series' four-color, accessible format makes the books attractive and inviting to readers of all levels. In addition, each viewpoint has been carefully edited to maximize a reader's understanding of the content. Short but thorough viewpoints capture the essence of an argument. A substantial, thought-provoking essay question placed at the end of each viewpoint asks the student to further investigate the issues raised in the viewpoint, compare and contrast two authors' arguments, or consider how one might go about forming an opinion on the topic at hand. Each viewpoint contains sidebars that include at-a-glance information and handy statistics. A Facts About section located in the back of the book further supplies students with relevant facts and figures.

Following in the tradition of the Opposing Viewpoints series, Greenhaven Press continues to provide readers with invaluable exposure to the controversial issues that shape our world. As John Stuart Mill once wrote: "The only way in which a human being can make some approach to knowing the whole of a subject is by hearing what can be said about it by persons of every variety of opinion and studying all modes in which it can be looked at by every character of mind. No wise man ever acquired his wisdom in any mode but this." It is to this principle that Introducing Issues with Opposing Viewpoints books are dedicated.

Introduction

"Despite all our efforts as a society to stop the use of illicit drugs, people are using them anyway, and it seems unlikely this situation is going to change soon."

—Dance Safe

"Drug users, like any other member of society, must be held accountable for their actions. Illicit drug use must bring swift and cost-effective consequences which will benefit the user and society at large."

—Drug Watch International

Despite decades of efforts against it, drug abuse continues to be a problem in America. In addition to being a health problem, it is a cause of crime, poverty, domestic violence, homelessness, and helps spread diseases such as HIV/AIDS. Yet while there is agreement that drug abuse is a problem, there is disagreement about how best to prevent it and treat the societal problems caused by it. When people consider ways to approach the problem of drug abuse, they usually end up discussing two opposing methods: "harm reduction" and "zero tolerance." Examining these two schools of thought is important to understanding the problem of drug abuse in America today.

The harm-reduction approach to drug abuse assumes that some people will use drugs no matter what. Therefore, it is believed that instead of trying to harshly penalize drug users and stubbornly eradicate all drug use, addicts should be treated in ways which reduce their harm to society and themselves. Needle-exchange programs are a good example of harm-reduction policies in the United States. In these programs, addicts are encouraged not necessarily to stop using drugs but to make sure they use them safely. Because it is difficult to completely stop heroin and other intravenous-drug use, needle-exchange programs seek to at least provide users with clean needles in order to lower the rate of HIV/AIDS and other diseases that spread quickly among

Volunteers of the Chicago Recovery Alliance distribute clean hypodermic needles and supplies to intravenous drug users.

intravenous-drug users when they share or use dirty needles. Researcher Don Des Jarlais of Beth Israel Medical Center in New York has tracked HIV among injection-drug users since the 1980s. According to Des Jarlais, needle-exchange programs "have played a critical role in stemming HIV/AIDS infections. There would be tens of thousands more people with HIV/AIDS in New York City if not for syringe exchanges." For these reasons, harm-reduction policies are championed as a realistic, practical, and humane way of helping drug users overcome their addiction. Alan Marlett, director of the University of Washington Addictive Behaviors Research Center says of such policies, "The idea is to reduce harm by degrees and just a few can make a big difference."

Opponents of these policies, however, are uncomfortable with giving the impression that any type of drug use is acceptable. They therefore support a set of policies that are described as "zero-tolerance," which treat drug abuse as a serious crime that deserves punishment. The zero-tolerance approach focuses on reducing the supply of drugs and creating a drug-free society by sending a clear, strong message that no form of drug use is to be tolerated. Like harm-reduction advocates, zero-tolerance advocates also believe in preventative and treatment-based educational programs to get people off drugs. However, zero-tolerance treatment programs demand abstinence. "To ask a recovered addict to engage in 'responsible heroin shooting' is to ignore the whole psychology and physiology of addiction," says psychologist James Royce. Zero-tolerance advocates firmly oppose any strategy which implies that there are safe or responsible ways to use drugs. As written in a February 2005 statement by the International Task Force on Strategic Drug Policy, "It is insufficient, illogical, and inhumane to proclaim that drug dependence should be maintained in the name of so-called 'harm reduction.' History, science, and reason tell us that drug use can be prevented, and drug dependence can be overcome and its attendant consequences reduced, if not eliminated."

While policy makers, substance-abuse counselors, scientists, and others debate the best way to approach the issue, drug abuse

Police in Maryland arrest a man for possession of illegal drugs.

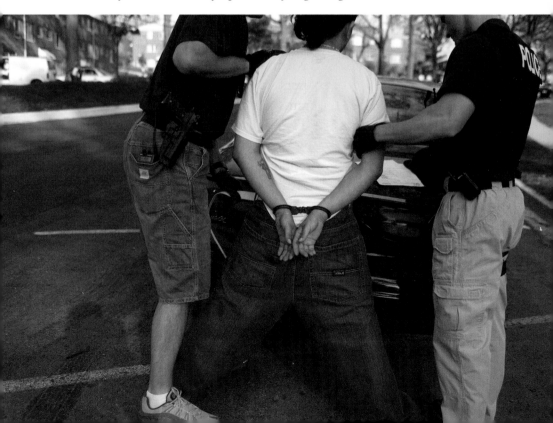

continues to be a problem for users, their family and friends, and for society. The viewpoints presented in *Introducing Issues with Opposing Viewpoints: Drug Abuse* offer further insight into the key aspects of this problem by exploring the scope of the drug-abuse crisis, how drug abuse can be prevented, the effectiveness of the war on drugs, and whether or not certain drugs should be legal.

Chapter 1

Is There a Drug Abuse Crisis?

A drug addict prepares to inject himself with heroin.

Viewpoint

1

Teen Drug Abuse Is a National Crisis

Meredith Maran

"In turn-of-the-millennium America more teenagers are using drugs than ever in the history of this country."

Meredith Maran says that in spite of the fact that society seems to be doing everything it can to prevent teenage drug abuse, more kids are using drugs than ever before. Maran supplies statistics on teenage drug abuse to support her claim. She contends that teenage drug abusers continue to abuse drugs into adulthood and the number of users increases annually. Maran believes the government has been unable to stop the epidemic and that more money should be spent on treatment rather than law enforcement. Maran is a journalist and has authored several books.

AS YOU READ, CONSIDER THE FOLLOWING QUESTIONS:

1. What percent of teens admit to smoking pot by their senior year in high school?
2. How many people are in treatment for drug or alcohol abuse on a typical day in America, according to the author?
3. For what does Maran say is the majority of the money that is budgeted for the president's "War on Drugs" used?

Meredith Maran, *Dirty: A Search for Answers Inside America's Teenage Drug Epidemic,* New York, NY: Harpers San Francisco, 2003. Copyright © 2003 by Meredith Maran. All rights reserved. Reproduced by permission of HarperCollins Publishers Inc.

America's drug crisis is a runaway train. Keeping teenagers from jumping on board—or being flattened on the tracks—is the linchpin of the nation's efforts to stop it. Research shows that if you don't use drugs as a kid, you're less likely to use drugs as an adult. Keeping teens clean today, the logic goes, equals fewer adult addicts tomorrow. The strategy is a reasonable one. The problem is, it hasn't worked.

Nothing Working

Despite countless attempts by governments, schools, churches, and families to contain the epidemic of teen drug use that exploded across the nation during the 1960s, the epidemic has been escalating (with an occasional downward blip) ever since. Thirty years into the government's multi-billion-dollar campaign to steer kids away from drugs and fifteen years since we were all mesmerized by that single egg frying in the pan—"This is your brain. This is your brain on drugs"—

Some feel that drug awareness programs, such as Drug Abuse Resistance Education (DARE), do not prevent young people from experimenting with drugs.

in turn-of-the-millennium America more teenagers are using drugs than ever in the history of this country, or any country in the world.

One-fourth of the high-school seniors in America today have problems with drugs and alcohol. Nearly two-thirds of the teenagers in America today do drugs before they finish high school—one-third of them by the time they're in eighth grade. (Do the math: we're talking twelve-year-olds.) Fifty-six percent of seventeen-year-olds know at least one drug dealer at school.

Nothing we're doing about it is working. Not the ads, not the DARE programs in the schools, not the after-school specials on TV. Not the glitzy rehab spas, the grimy public treatment centers, the fancy boarding schools. Not the Juvenile Halls, the youth detention camps, the jails.

Teen Drug Use Alarmingly High

By the time they're seniors in high school:

- 50 percent of teenagers have binged on alcohol (chugged five or more drinks in a row).
- 41 percent have smoked pot.
- 12.5 percent have taken tranquilizers or barbiturates.
- 12 percent have taken Ecstasy ("X" use was up 71 percent between 1999 and 2001).
- 11 percent have used amphetamines ("speed" in its various forms).
- 10 percent have taken LSD.
- 9 percent have used cocaine, about half in the form of crack.
- 9 percent have sniffed inhalants.
- 4 percent have snorted or shot heroin.

Two hundred thousand American teenagers were arrested for drug violations in 1999, an increase of 291 percent over the past decade. Seven out of ten juveniles who get in trouble with the law test positive for drugs. Nine out of ten teenagers who need drug treatment aren't getting it.

These are your kids. These are your kids on drugs.

Number One Health Problem

Welcome to America, where on any given day, one million people are in treatment for drug or alcohol abuse. The number one health problem in the nation, substance abuse causes more death and illness than

Andy Singer. © Andy Singer. Reproduced by permission of Cagle Cartoons, Inc.

any other preventable condition. Four times as many women die from addiction-related illness, for example, as die from breast cancer.

Nearly fifteen million Americans—6.3 percent of the population

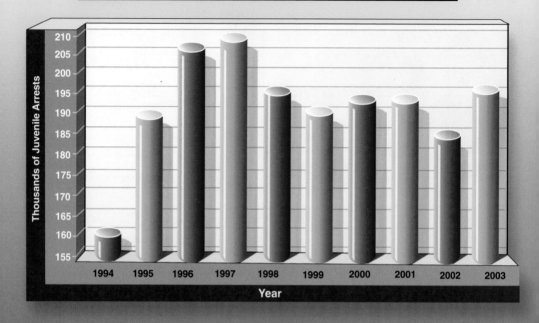

Number of Teen Drug Arrests, 1994–2003

Source: Department of Justice, Federal Bureau of Investigation, Special reports: Arrest of Juveniles for Drug Arrest Violations from 1994 to 2003.

age twelve and over—are illicit-drug users. Half of them are under age twenty-six. All told, they spend $60 billion a year on the illegal stuff they smoke, snort, swallow, and shoot.

U.S. Prisons Are Burgeoning with Drug Users

Whether you indulge or not, you're paying for the party. Drug abuse costs the U.S. economy $414 billion a year. Besides the health and productivity costs, President Bush's War on Drugs swallows $19.2 billion. Two-thirds of that is spent on law enforcement and interdiction (kicking in housing-project doors, making sure the people who get busted go to jail). With no apparent comprehension of cause and effect—only 3.6 percent of the War on Drugs budget is allotted for treatment, 2.4 percent for prevention—the Bush administration acknowledges that most people who need treatment aren't getting it.

More than one million people a year are arrested for drugs, contributing generously to one of our nation's most dubious achievements: the United States has the second-highest—and the fastest-growing—incarceration rate in the world. Sixty percent of the nearly two million people in our prisons today are drug offenders. If the prison population keeps increasing at its current rate (6.6 million Americans—one in every thirty-two adults—are currently incarcerated, on probation, or on parole), by 2053 there will be more Americans in jail than out.

This is your country. This is your country on drugs.

EVALUATING THE AUTHORS' ARGUMENTS:

In this viewpoint the author sounds an alarm about drugs pervading the lives of teenagers. She argues that the government and schools cannot stop teenage drug abuse. She does not offer any solutions to the problem. How does this affect your opinions of her article?

A Teen Drug Abuse Crisis Does Not Exist

Drug Reform Coordination Network

"Teenage drug use is the least of our problems."

In this viewpoint Mike Males argues that groups such as the Office of National Drug Control Policy (ONDCP) and the Partnership for a Drug Free America are continuously reporting on some teenage drug epidemic or another, when in reality they do not exist. Teens are being scapegoated, says Males. The real drug problem in America today is drug abuse by adults. Males is a sociologist at the University of California at Santa Cruz and a columnist for the newsletter *Youth Today*.

AS YOU READ, CONSIDER THE FOLLOWING QUESTIONS:
1. Which drug-use surveys does Males think are reliable?
2. Which drugs does Males classify as "soft drugs"?
3. What is the basis for Males's claim that teen drug abuse is much rarer today than it was thirty years ago?

"DRCNET Interview: Youth Sociologist Mike Males," *Drug War Chronicles, www.stopthedrugwar.com,* November 21, 2003. Reproduced by permission.

The drug war has prospered—despite its massive failure to stem drug abuse after spending hundreds of billions of dollars and arresting 13 million people over the past 20 years—by constantly whipping up fears of adolescents. Nearly every ONDCP [Office of National Drug Control Policy], Partnership for a Drug-Free America, and CASA [Center on Addiction and Substance Abuse] press release today claims a massive, conveniently hidden teenage drug crisis—the crisis rotates from coke to pot to heroin to meth to ecstasy to Oxycontin, etc.—terrible scourges they claim parents would be terrified of if they knew about them.

The teen drug crisis does not exist. I've investigated nearly every one of them. There is no evidence of teenage deaths, hospital ER cases, or even addiction-related crime by youths that would be obvious if any real youth drug abuse epidemic existed. Rather, it is fear of some imagined youth crisis that drives the war on drugs. . . .

Distorted Claims

Unfortunately, several drug policy reform groups have issued public statements reinforcing the drug war's distorted claim that teens are suffering some kind of drug abuse crisis and agreeing that stopping teens from using any drug should be our drug policy's overriding goal. This is not simply dishonest, it's a politically insane strategy for reformers to pursue. What they are saying is that marijuana is so dangerous to teens that we should marshal the drug war to enforce absolute teen prohibition. Bizarrely, they somehow think this tactic will build support for their nonsensical claim that legalizing marijuana for adults will stop teens from getting it.

These groups comb dozens of surveys (including ones such as CASA's and PRIDE's [Parents Resource Institute for Drug Education] that are completely biased and unreliable) that measure use of dozens of drugs across multiple adolescent

> **FAST FACT**
>
> According to the University of Michigan's 2005 *Monitoring the Future* survey, there has been a 19 percent decline in overall drug use among eighth, tenth, and twelfth graders since 2001.

Whether parents should be more concerned about teens smoking than abusing illegal drugs is subject to debate.

groups and drug-use categories such as lifetime, monthly, etc.—hundreds of numbers each year, which always show some drugs are being used a bit more and some a bit less—in order to selectively ferret out any increase in teen use, no matter how insignificant. They then issue alarmist press releases alleging huge increases in this or that category of teenage coke or heroin or pot use and blaming the drug war for failing to "protect our children." Those kind of emotional, prohibitionist scare tactics are exactly what we condemn drug warriors for exploiting.

Meanwhile, 200 separate surveys by more reliable entities such as Monitoring the Future and the National Household Survey show without exception that teens find legal drugs such as alcohol and tobacco far easier to get, and use them far more, than illegal drugs. The best information is that if we legalize marijuana, a few more teens and adults will use it, and that is no cause for panic. Surveys clearly show strong correlations between adult drinking, smoking, and marijuana use—where adults use a lot, so do teens. . . .

We Should Stop Focusing on Teens

Youths have already demonstrated that they know the difference between hard and soft drugs. The vast majority of teen drug use today consists of (a) beer, (b) social, that is, weekend or occasional, cigarette smoking, (c) marijuana, and (d) ecstasy. They use softer drugs in more moderate quantities than adults do. That is why so few teens are dying from drugs or getting addicted. It is a major irony that today's adolescents already follow the very model of "harm reduction" that

Some argue that teens abuse alcohol far more than illegal drugs.

Teens dance at a rave. Whether teen drug abuse is a serious problem is a hotly debated issue.

drug reform groups want to see society as a whole adopt, and yet we insist on depicting the teens as in some kind of terrible danger.

Trying to scare the public about teens is not just useless. The whole scheme of focusing on teenage drug use is just plain crazy for drug reformers. This country will never legalize pot as long as it remains so frightened of its youth and ready to believe any terrible thing any self-interest group says. In fact, teenage drug use is the least of our problems. We need to turn down the heat on this issue. Drug reform groups need to go back to basic honesty—drug abuse (not use) is the problem, older (not younger) groups are suffering from addiction crises, the drug war's diversionary distortions about teens and its punitive policies have only made these worse, and it's time to spell out why America is caught up in its worst drug abuse crisis in history right now—record peaks in hospitalizations and deaths from illegal drugs, as well as drug-related imprisonments, in 2001 and 2002. The worst crisis is a very real, gigantic increase in drug abuse by hundreds of thousands of older-agers—mostly white folks—that no one will talk about precisely because our real drug abusers are higher status, main-stream populations. . . .

Teen drug use goes up and down, but teen drug abuse (in terms of overdose deaths) is far rarer today than it was 30 years ago, and far lower than middle-aged drug abuse today. Drug reform groups should stop trying to exploit fear of teenagers and just state the facts: Teens are not the drug problem, teenage use of marijuana is not a serious issue, and teens are far more endangered by the drug war's dereliction in preventing manifest drug abuse among their parents and other adults than they are by their own adolescent drug experimentation. . . .

We should have confidence in teens' judgment and learn from them. Teens are using milder drugs (beer, marijuana, ecstasy) in safer settings than adults, which is why teens suffer so few overdoses and deaths today. Of 20,000 drug overdose deaths in 2000, just 475 were under age 20—16,000 were over age 30. Leave teens alone. Look instead at drug abuse by their parents, whose bad example of heroin, cocaine, meth, mixed-drug, and alcohol combined with drug abuse is the best (and most painful) education of the younger generation against hard drug abuse ever.

EVALUATING THE AUTHORS' ARGUMENTS:

Contrast Males's viewpoint with the previous viewpoint by Maran. Which viewpoint was more persuasive and why? Cite two facts from the one you found most convincing.

Methamphetamine Abuse Is a Crisis in the United States

National Association of Counties

"The meth epidemic is a complex problem that is not easily solved."

In this viewpoint the National Association of Counties (NACo) contends that a methamphetamine (meth) epidemic rages across the United States from the West Coast to the East Coast. NACo bases their contention on a survey of police officers and child welfare workers from all over the country. NACo says that meth addicts are stealing and committing other serious crimes in order to finance their drug habits and meth-addicted parents are endangering their children. The organization represents county governments across the nation in Washington D.C.

AS YOU READ, CONSIDER THE FOLLOWING QUESTIONS:

1. How many pounds of toxic waste are produced for each pound of methamphetamine, as reported by NACo?
2. According to NACo, what crimes are increasing because of the use of methamphetamine?
3. Methamphetamine affects what system of the body?

The methamphetamine epidemic in the United States, which began in the West and is moving East, is having a devastating effect on our country. The increasingly widespread production, distribution and use of meth are now affecting urban, suburban and rural communities nationwide. County governments across America are on the front lines in responding to the methamphetamine crisis.

For counties, meth abuse causes legal, medical, environmental and social problems. County governments and their citizens must pay for investigating and closing meth labs, making arrests, holding lawbreakers in detention centers and then trying them, providing treatment for those addicted to the drug, and cleaning-up lab sites.

There are also many societal effects that must be considered. In an alarming number of meth arrests, there is a child living in the home. These children many times suffer from neglect and abuse.

Meth labs pose a significant danger in the community, as they contain highly flammable and explosive materials. Additionally, for each pound of methamphetamine produced, five to seven pounds of toxic waste remain, which is often introduced into the environment via streams, septic systems and surface water run-off.

> **FAST FACT**
>
> According to the Substance Abuse and Mental Health Services Administration (SAMHSA), from 1993 to 2003 the number of people receiving treatment for methamphetamine addiction increased fourfold.

The meth epidemic is a complex problem that is not easily solved. To better understand the extent of the problem, the National Association of Counties (NACo) recently conducted surveys of law enforcement and county child welfare officials in order to determine the impact of meth on these county services and their communities. . . .

Meth and Crime

Crime and police activities have increased in response to meth growth. As the numbers of people who used meth grew and the numbers of

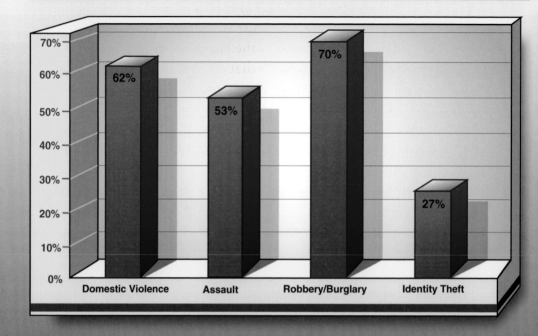

The Meth Epidemic in America. Washington, DC: National Association of Counties, July 5, 2005.

people who became addicted to meth grew, police involvement also grew. Meth users were criminals who committed other crimes while under the influence of the drug and also to finance the purchase or manufacture of the drug. County law enforcement officials began to see a dramatic increase in the number of arrests that involved this drug. . . .

On the national level, the federal government still considers marijuana as the number one drug problem in America, but county law enforcement officials have a different perspective on this ranking. With the growth of this drug [i.e., methamphetamine] from the rural areas of the western and northwestern regions of this country and its slow but continuing spread to the east, local law enforcement officials see it as their number one drug problem. . . .

Although the use of methamphetamines is itself a crime, there are several other crimes that have been increasing because of the prolific use of this drug. Seventy percent of the responding officials say that robberies or burglaries have increased because of meth use, while 62 percent report increases in domestic violence. In addition, simple assaults (53%) and identity thefts (27%) have also increased. . . .

As a means of waging a war against the methamphetamine epidemic, many counties are targeting the labs that are built to manufacture the drug. Many of the labs that remain in this country are small labs, and are often portable. Although toxic and dangerous to the environment, they have been flourishing in recent years. Sixty two percent of the county law enforcement officials report that lab seizures have increased in their counties in the last 3 years. In the Lower Midwest, 74% report increases in lab seizures, while 68% of counties in the Upper Midwest report increases. Even the Northeast, where very few county officials rank meth as the number one drug problem, reports a 42% increase in lab seizures during the last 3 years. . . .

Meth and Children

There are many innocent victims of the increased use of methamphetamines in this country. To understand who they are, it is important to look at the drug's effects. Meth is favored by many drug users because it alters their moods. Since there are several ways that the drug can be taken, its effects will differ based on the method used. If smoked or taken by intravenous injection, there is an intense high that lasts for just a few minutes but has been compared to crack in its pleasure. Smoking or injecting will give the fastest high, sometimes in as little as 5 to 10 seconds. The high from snorting or eating the drug does not produce the intense rush that other methods do.

The drug, which stimulates the central nervous system, can create effects that can last for nearly an entire day. It modifies the behavior of the users, and after lengthy use it can actually change the way the brain functions. Meth has been known to cause heart failure, brain damage and stroke. It is also responsible for many psychological changes in the user. These psychological affects can cause anger, panic, paranoia, hallucinations, repetitive behavior, confusion, jerky or flailing movements, irritability, insomnia, aggression, incessant talking and convulsions. Many of these side effects can lead to violent aggressive acts and suicide.

Now add a child to this volatile mixture. Pregnancies of methamphetamine-addicted mothers can produce birth defects, low

Chris Slane. Reproduced by permission of Cagle Cartoons, Inc.

birth weight, attention deficit disorder, and other behavior disorders. In addition, the side effects of the drug that are affecting the parents create a greater risk of child abuse, shaken baby syndrome and neglect.

As law enforcement officials are clamping down on the manufacture and use of meth, they are finding a disturbing side effect. Many children are being grossly neglected by their addicted parents and these same children are being exposed to the harmful side effects of the production of the drug if they live in close proximity to a lab. . . .

Children who are the victims of the methamphetamine epidemic are presenting many unique challenges to social service workers, foster parents, counselors and adoption workers. As a result, 69% of the responding officials from county social service agencies indicate that their counties have had to provide additional and special training for their welfare system workers and have had to develop new and special protocols for workers to address the special needs of these displaced children.

EVALUATING THE AUTHORS' ARGUMENTS:

This viewpoint's conclusions are based on the results of a survey of law enforcement personnel. Do you think that survey results provide a good basis for a viewpoint? What other groups of people might you want to survey to decide whether a meth epidemic exists in the United States?

Methamphetamine Abuse Is Not a Crisis in the United States

Steve Chapman

"A lot of people are 'crying meth' because it's a hot new drug."

The methamphetamine epidemic described in the previous viewpoint is all hype, says Steve Chapman, a columnist for the *Chicago Tribune*. In this viewpoint Chapman says drug war champions are always exaggerating the harms of one drug or another, and meth is the latest drug receiving the hype. He questions some of the claims of the National Association of Counties and other groups, who shrilly claim that meth abuse is racing across the country wreaking havoc on American communities. Chapman says the government is reacting in typical drug war fashion too, and whatever they are doing to try to curb the use of methamphetamine will not work anyway.

AS YOU READ, CONSIDER THE FOLLOWING QUESTIONS:
1. Name two other drugs Chapman says were "hyped" in the name of the drug war.
2. What is the addiction rate for methamphetamine compared to tobacco or alcohol?
3. What is a primary ingredient in homemade meth, as reported by Chapman?

'America's Most Dangerous Drug,' blares the cover story in *Newsweek*. If you haven't been paying attention, you might wonder what drug the magazine has in mind.

Tobacco, which kills more than 400,000 people each year? Alcohol, which contributes to thousands of traffic fatalities? Crack, which spawned a wave of violent crime in the 1990s? Heroin, which was supposedly an epidemic a few years ago?

Meth Is Latest Drug War Monster

Answer: None of the above. America's most dangerous drug of the week is methamphetamine, better known as crystal meth. It may sound odd that this new scourge is more hazardous than all those other drugs, which have not gotten any less malignant. But the drug war is sort of

Some reports on the harmful effects of methamphetamine (pictured) are contested.

like horror movies: A new monster is always needed, and the new monster is never much different from the old one.

Crystal meth is blamed for all sorts of ills. Addicts allegedly neglect their children, beat their spouses, rot out their teeth, ruin their health, commit burglaries and accidentally set themselves on fire in crude home laboratories. All of this may be true. But we've heard similar lurid tales about other drugs—none of which quite lived up to the hype.

Once it was marijuana. Then heroin. Later, the unstoppable menace was cocaine. A 1983 *Time* magazine story had this passage: "Several times last year Phil stood quivering and feverish in the living room, his loaded pistol pointed toward imaginary enemies. . . . Rita, emaciated like her husband, had her own bogeymen—strangers with X-ray vision." A prosecutor said, "An exceptionally violent streak seems to run through the trade." Sound like another drug you've heard about lately?

But drug epidemics are not like contagious diseases. Illicit substances don't infect people against their will—people make choices about whether to use them. When a substance is truly destructive, word gets around, and people turn away. Toothless addicts with horrible burns and oozing sores are not going to seduce hordes of eager young recruits. In time, the meth epidemic will play itself out.

Crying "Wolf" About Meth

It's not even clear, though, that there is an epidemic. The federal Substance Abuse and Mental Health Services Administration [SAMHSA] which does a huge annual survey on drug use, says that in 2003, the last year for which it has data, there was no increase in methamphetamine use from the previous year. If it's spreading in some places, it's losing ground elsewhere.

Nor is meth all that addictive. SAMHSA reports that 5.2 percent of all Americans age 12 and older have tried the drug at least once.

Some argue that tobacco and alcohol are more addictive than methamphetamine.

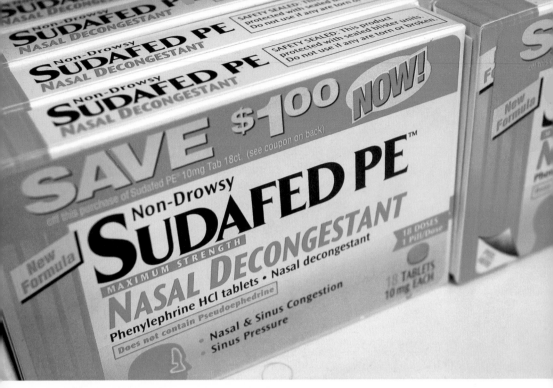

Some companies have changed the formulas of their medicines so they cannot be converted to methamphetamine.

But only 0.3 percent are currently using it. That means the addiction rate is no more than 1 in 17. The addiction rate for tobacco, by contrast, is more than 1 in 3. For alcohol, it's about one in 12.

Maybe that's why even some members of the Bush administration are rolling their eyes. A spokesman for the White House Office of National Drug Control Policy complained to *Newsweek* that a lot of people are "'crying meth' because it's a hot new drug."

Anti-Meth Tactics Are Not Working

But when a panic erupts, the government tends to fall back on old weapons, even if they haven't worked very well before. The fight against meth consists mainly of two approaches: seizing home labs where the drug is made and restricting sales of over-the-counter medicines that can be converted into the drug.

Neither holds much promise. If you crack down on production of meth here in America, users will look for sources elsewhere. Already, half of the stuff consumed here comes from Mexico.

Cold Medicine Crackdown

Recently, Oregon [and many other states] passed a law requiring a prescription for common over-the-counter drugs, like Sudafed, that contain pseudoephedrine, a primary ingredient in homemade meth. That will certainly inconvenience people with colds and allergies, who spend $1.4 billion a year on drugs containing pseudoephedrine. Some of them will have to pay for a doctor visit just to get a garden-variety remedy like Claritin-D or Alka-Seltzer Plus.

But will tighter controls curb drug abuse? Not likely. After Oklahoma passed a law requiring that pseudoephedrine drugs be sold only by pharmacists from behind the counter, it saw a 90 percent drop in lab seizures. Unfortunately, it was a dubious victory. Users didn't go straight but switched to meth smuggled from Mexico.

"Our problem hasn't gone away," Oklahoma City police Lt. Tom Terhune told The Associated Press. "The problem that's gone away is the meth labs."

The government can't save us from methamphetamine. But given the benefit of knowledge gained from sad experience, we can save ourselves.

EVALUATING THE AUTHORS' ARGUMENTS:

Considering what you know on the topic, what is your opinion on the reality of a meth epidemic? Do you believe it is hype, as the author of this viewpoint contends? Or do you believe the previous author's viewpoint that there is a serious meth epidemic spreading across the United States? Explain your point of view.

Viewpoint

5

Prescription Drug Abuse Is Reaching Crisis Proportions

Joseph Califano Jr.

"America is in a perfect storm of abuse of mind altering prescription drugs."

In this viewpoint Joseph Califano Jr. proclaims that prescription-drug abuse is the number one drug threat facing Americans, especially teenagers. Prescriptions for antidepressants, pain relievers, antianxiety drugs, and steroids have exploded in recent years. As a result, medicine cabinets full of these drugs are accessible to kids. In addition, the Internet is fueling the illegal distribution of drugs such as steroids and Oxycontin. Califano says more people abuse prescription drugs than cocaine, heroin, and hallucinogens combined, and prescription-drug abuse has the potential to rival alcohol and marijuana abuse.

Califano is the chairman of the National Center on Addiction and Substance Abuse (CASA), an organization that seeks to reduce drug abuse in the United States.

Joseph Califano, "Accompanying Statement for Under the Counter: The Diversion and Abuse of Controlled Prescription Drugs in the U.S.," *The National Center on Substance Abuse and Addiction at Columbia University*, July, 2005, p. I–IV. Reproduced by permission.

AS YOU READ, CONSIDER THE FOLLOWING QUESTIONS:
1. In Califano's view, what is driving the increase in prescription drug abuse?
2. What foreshadowed the increase in the abuse of prescription drugs, according to the author?
3. What is a "pharming" party, as described in the viewpoint?

While America has been congratulating itself in recent years on curbing increases in alcohol and illicit drug abuse and in the decline in teen smoking, abuse and addiction of controlled prescription drugs—opioids, central nervous system depressants and stimulants—have been stealthily, but sharply, rising. Between 1992 and 2003, while the U.S. population increased 14 percent, the number of people abusing controlled prescription drugs jumped 94 percent—twice the increase in the number of people abusing marijuana, five times in the number abusing cocaine and 60 times the increase in the number abusing heroin. Controlled prescription drugs like OxyContin, Ritalin

FAST FACT

According to the Center on Addiction and Substance Abuse (CASA), from 2004 to 2005 the percentage of teens who know a friend or classmate who has abused prescription drugs increased 86 percent.

and Valium are now the fourth most abused substance in America behind only marijuana, alcohol and tobacco.

Teens Abusing Prescription Drugs

Particularly alarming is the 212 percent increase from 1992 to 2003 in the number of 12- to 17-year olds abusing controlled prescription drugs, and the increasing number of teens trying these drugs for the first time. New abuse of prescription opioids among teens is up an astounding 542 percent, more than four times the rate of increase among adults. The explosion in the prescription of addictive opioids, depressants and stimulants has, for many children, made the medicine cabinet a greater temptation and threat than the illegal street drug

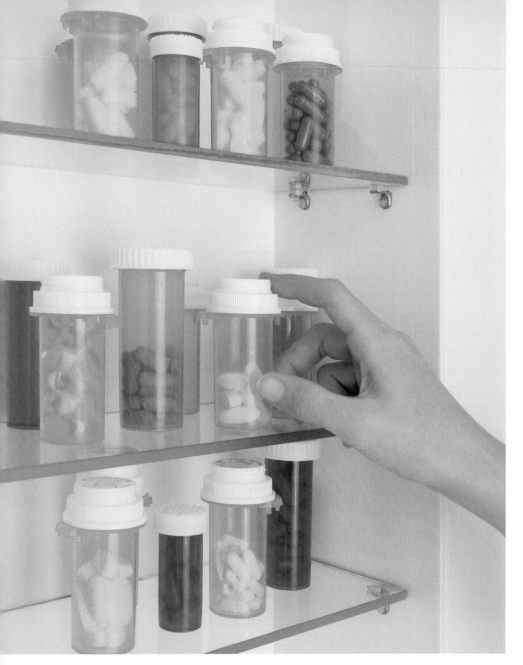

In recent years, teen prescription-drug abuse has risen significantly.

dealer, as some parents have become unwitting and passive pushers.

Teens who abuse controlled prescription drugs are twice as likely to use alcohol, five times likelier to use marijuana, 12 times likelier to use heroin, 15 times likelier to use Ecstasy, and 21 times likelier to use cocaine, compared to teens who do not abuse such drugs. . . .

Medicine Cabinets Provide Easy Access

America is in a perfect storm of abuse of mind altering prescription drugs including: opioids like OxyContin and Vicodin that relieve pain, central nervous system (CNS) depressants like Valium and Xanax that relieve anxiety, CNS stimulants like Ritalin, Adderall and Dexedrine that boost attention and energy, and steroids like Anadrol and Equipoise that enhance athletic performance. The question is why?

One factor driving the increase in controlled prescription drug abuse is that these drugs can be found in abundance in family medicine cabinets in every town in America, and they are just a click away on the Internet. They can be acquired with relative ease from doctors, friends, relatives and classmates. The fact that controlled prescription drugs are approved by the FDA and prescribed by a physician leads many to conclude that they are safe even when abused. Sadly, nothing could be further from the truth.

Prescription Drugs Far from Safe

Controlled prescription drug abuse can lead to serious emotional, social and health problems, medical emergencies and death. In 2002, controlled prescription drugs accounted for 23 percent of all drug-related emergency department mentions in the U.S. Between 1994 and 2002, there was a 168 percent increase in emergency department opioid mentions, four times more than the increase in cocaine mentions, three and a half times the increase in heroin mentions and exceeded only marginally by marijuana mentions (198 percent increase). In 2002, controlled prescription drug abuse was implicated in one in five emergency room deaths. The concurrent abuse of alcohol and illicit drugs by three-quarters of controlled prescription drug abusers further raises their risk of dangerous consequences.

The abuse of controlled prescription drugs was foreshadowed by dramatic increases in their manufacture and distribution and in the number of prescriptions written and filled. Between 1992 and 2002, while the U.S. population increased 13 percent and the number of prescriptions written for non-controlled drugs increased by 57 percent, the number of prescriptions filled for controlled drugs increased by 154 percent. During this same period, there was a 90 percent increase (from 7.8 million to 14.8 million) in the number of people who admitted abusing controlled prescription drugs—a 203 percent increase among 12- to 17-year olds and a 78 percent increase among those 18 and older (by 2003, the comparable increases were 212 percent for teens and 81 percent for adults).

In 1986 basketball star Len Bias (right) died of a cocaine overdose. Such well-publicized deaths increase public awareness of the dangers of drugs.

OxyContin and the Internet

As the overdose death of basketball star Len Bias awakened the nation in 1986 to the danger of cocaine, so the explosion in OxyContin prescriptions written to treat non-cancer pain—from 670,000 in 1997 to some 6.2 million in 2002—and the resulting rampant abuse and addiction related to the drug sounded the prescription drug alarm for many and drew attention to gaps in prevention and control.

For example, the Internet is a wide-open highway for distribution of illegally acquired abusable prescription drugs. An investigation conducted for this report by Beau Dietl & Associates found hundreds of Web sites advertising and selling controlled prescription opioids, CNS depressants, CNS stimulants and steroids. Most could be purchased without a prescription and without regard to age, so teens and children could easily get them. A little Internet savvy and a credit card were the only requirements to have the drugs arrive at the designated address within a few days. . . .

Pharmaceutical companies may contribute to diversion and abuse by the way they formulate and market controlled drugs. The abuse potential of a drug is linked to the speed and intensity of the high it creates. Drugs like OxyContin and Dilaudid that can easily be altered to destroy their time-release mechanism are premium on the abuse market. Yet, formulation of a drug to reduce its abuse potential is not a required consideration by either pharmaceutical companies or the Food and Drug Administration (FDA) in bringing a controlled drug to market. Nor are plans to manage the risk of diversion and abuse required for all controlled drugs prior to their release. Aggressive marketing of controlled drugs to physicians—as occurred with OxyContin for moderate as well as severe pain—is designed to increase profits with little regard for abuse potential. In recent years pharmaceutical companies have begun to market controlled prescription drugs directly to consumers in order to increase demand.

Parents and Doctors Play a Key Role

Controlled prescription drugs can be stolen anywhere along the pathway from manufacture to consumption and diverted for illicit use by individuals or criminal operations. CASA's surveys of physicians and pharmacists reveal that both believe the major source of diversion is

Some prescription-drug abusers convince doctors to write prescriptions for drugs they do not need.

patients through such techniques as doctor shopping, fraudulent or altered prescriptions, and deception and manipulation of doctors.

But parents also play a key role. Their easily accessible medicine cabinets containing these very drugs are an open invitation to children—fueling "pharming" parties where teens bring drugs from home and trade or share for purposes of getting high. Parental ignorance about the dangers of these drugs and failure to safeguard them (e.g., by locking their medicine cabinets) can yield inadvertent but devastating harm to their own children.

With the rapid pace of development of new mood-altering pharmaceuticals and with abuse and addiction climbing so sharply, controlled prescription drug abuse has the potential to rival alcohol and marijuana abuse. Avoiding such an outcome requires an all-fronts effort of prevention and control. The task of eliminating diversion and abuse cannot be left to law enforcement alone, for even the most well funded and staffed enforcement efforts cannot succeed on their own. Parents, physicians, pharmacists, pharmaceutical companies, schools and public health officials must sign up.

EVALUATING THE AUTHORS' ARGUMENTS:

Califano has said that he wrote this article in the hope of waking people up to an impending prescription-drug-abuse epidemic. Do you think his arguments are persuasive enough to sound an alarm about prescription drug abuse? What groups of people do you think he directed his message at, and why?

Chapter 2

How Can Drug Abuse Be Reduced?

Demonstrators who favor the legalization of marijuana gather at the University of Michigan in 2002.

Viewpoint 1

The War on Drugs Reduces Drug Abuse

Jonathan V. Last

"While no one was paying attention, America has been winning its war on drugs."

The "War on Drugs" was first coined by President Richard M. Nixon to refer to the government strategy to carry out an "all-out offensive" to eradicate drug supply and drug use. The drug war encompasses everything from antidrug television ads to drug laws and foreign policy. In this viewpoint Jonathan Last says the drug war has been a quiet success. He claims that both the supply of drugs and teen drug abuse have been reduced because of it.

Last is the online editor of the conservative magazine *Weekly Standard*. He also writes a weekly editorial for the *Philadelphia Inquirer*.

AS YOU READ, CONSIDER THE FOLLOWING QUESTIONS:
1. In what year did the percent of 12- to 17-year-olds who had used drugs shrink to 16.4 percent, according to Last?
2. Why, in the author's opinion, is so much attention given to drug-use statistics for 12- to 17- and 18- to 25-year-olds?
3. What is one reason given for the decline in drug use after 2001?

There's a wonderful scene in the movie *Traffic* in which a captured drug kingpin, played by Miguel Ferrer, is being interrogated by two federal agents. Ferrer says to them disdainfully: "You people are like those Japanese soldiers left behind on deserted islands who think that World War II is still going on. Let me be the first to tell you, your government surrendered this war a long time ago."

It's a brilliant bit of filmmaking; it's also bunk. Over the last five years, while no one was paying attention, America has been winning its war on drugs.

The cosmopolitan view has long been that the fight against drugs is a losing battle; that the supply of drugs pouring into America is never-ending; that drug lords are unrelenting zombie-supermen—kill one, and five more spring up.

Reduced Teen Drug Use

The American drug problem grew to epidemic proportions throughout the 1960s and 1970s. In 1979, agencies of Health and Human

Some argue that teen drug abuse has decreased in recent years.

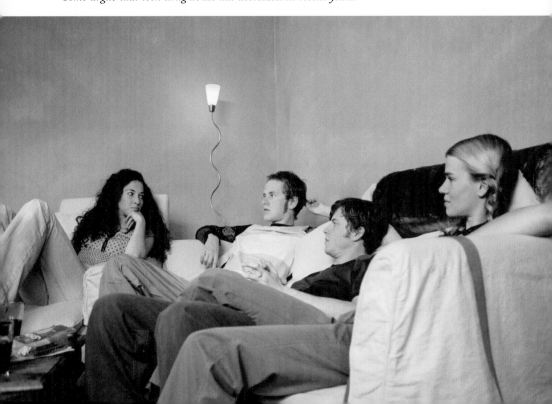

Services and the National Institutes of Health performed a national household survey of illicit drug use; substances included marijuana, cocaine, heroin, banned hallucinogens and inhalants, and unauthorized use of sedatives, stimulants and analgesics. As of 1979, the numbers were horrifying: 31.8 percent of teens ages 12 to 17 had used drugs; 16.3 percent of them had used in the last month. Among those ages 18 to 25 it was worse: 69 percent had used at some point; 38 percent in the last month.

But throughout the '80s, those numbers shrank. Sophisticates derided "Just Say No," but by 1993, only 16.4 percent of 12- to 17-year-olds had used, and only 5.7 percent had used in the last month. In the 18-to-25 age bracket, 50.2 percent had tried drugs, but only 15 percent had used in the last 30 days. It was a remarkable success.

From 1993 to 2001, the numbers become less rosy: Among ages 12 to 17, the percentage of youths who had tried drugs increased almost twofold. In the 18-to-25 crowd, the increase was less marked, but still noticeable.

There's a reason we pay so much attention to these two age groups. As Tom Riley, the director of public affairs at the Office of National Drug Control Policy (ONDCP), explains:

> **FAST FACT**
>
> According to the Office of National Drug Control Policy (ONDCP), by pursuing a strategy focusing on prevention and treatment, as well as law enforcement and international programs, there were six hundred thousand fewer teens using drugs in 2005 than there were in 2001.

"If people don't start using drugs as teenagers—the mechanism of addiction clicks much more quickly in the developing brain—then they are unlikely to ever go on to serious drug abuse. If we can reduce the number of teens who use drugs, we change the shape of the problem for generations to come."

After 2001, the tide turned again. Since then, teen drug use is off nearly 19 percent. Which means that 700,000 fewer teens are using drugs today than just a few years ago.

What happened? For one thing: funding. Since 1998, the ONDCP's real budget has increased, from $8.2 billion to $12.4 billion. That extra money has mostly gone to law enforcement and drug treatment,

Bolivian soldiers walk past a coca drying area in the town of Chapare in 2001. Coca production around the world has decreased due to efforts to destroy coca fields.

attacking both the supply and the demand sides of the problem. Measures for demand are fuzzy, but the supply side of the equation—the "war" part of the war on drugs—has solid metrics.

Each substance is its own front and has its own dynamics. Drug supply is shockingly local. Take coca, the substance from which cocaine and crack are derived. From 1998 to 2001, world coca production increased from 586,100 metric tons to 655,800 metric tons, with the lion's share grown in Columbia. Since then, the ONDCP orchestrated a campaign to spray 140,000 hectares of Colombian coca fields with glyphosate (you know it as Roundup). The result: world coca production is down 20 percent.

With other substances, the news is even better. On Nov. 6, 2000, the Drug Enforcement Agency raided an abandoned missile silo in Wamego, Kan., which housed the world's leading LSD operation. By 2004, LSD availability in America was down 95 percent. The market still hasn't recovered.

The supply of all the major drugs is down, but at the same time, drug interdiction is up. In 1989, 533,533 kilograms of the four major drugs were seized by U.S. authorities. By 2005, the total had risen to 1.3 million kilograms. . . .

Quiet Success

[ONDCP] director John Walters is not the type to go running for the nearest TV camera. Yet the quiet success he has overseen is a powerful reminder that the bad guys are not 10 feet tall; that failure is not inevitable; that the war on drugs is a war worth fighting; and that we're fighting it well.

EVALUATING THE AUTHORS' ARGUMENTS:

This viewpoint, as well as many others, includes various statistics. Do you find statistics to be persuasive? Do you think some statistics are more valid than others? Can statistics be used deceptively? Explain your answer.

Viewpoint 2

The War on Drugs Does Not Reduce Drug Abuse

"With each passing year of this continuing war, the 'drug problem' has become exponentially more dreadful."

Jack Cole

Jack Cole is a retired narcotics officer and a member of the organization Law Enforcement Against Prohibition (LEAP). Cole says that since its inception the war on drugs has been a big bureaucratic machine that has led law enforcement officers and the government to tell lies to justify its existence. The war on drugs was supposed to reduce drug-related deaths, diseases, crimes, and addiction. However, Cole maintains that drug use increased and drug users switched to harder drugs because of the war on drugs. The war on drugs has been an abject failure, he concludes.

AS YOU READ, CONSIDER THE FOLLOWING QUESTIONS:
1. According to Cole, what are four unintended consequences of the war on drugs?
2. What did the 2002 Monitoring the Future study find about teen marijuana use, according to Cole?
3. What program did Switzerland start in 1994?

Jack Cole, "End Prohibition Now," *Law Enforcement Against Prohibition*, September 21, 2005, p. 1–8. Reproduced by permission.

After retiring from a 26-year career in law enforcement, where I served 12 years as an undercover narcotics officer, I helped found Law Enforcement Against Prohibition (LEAP). LEAP is a 5,000 member international educational organization created to give voice to law-enforcers who believe the war on drugs is a policy of failure and destruction. The police, judges, prosecutors, prison wardens, DEA and FBI agents who are members of LEAP know ending

Andy Singer. © Andy Singer. Reproduced by permission of Cagle Cartoons, Inc.

drug prohibition is a more efficient and ethical way to lower the incidence of death, disease, crime and addiction, than fighting a war on drugs.

With each passing year of this continuing war, the "drug problem" has become exponentially more dreadful.

Unintended Consequences

(1) *Drugs are more plentiful.* In 1970 one ounce seizures of heroin were considered large but by 2002 law enforcement made individual seizures of ten tons of heroin and twenty tons of cocaine.

(2) *Drugs are more potent and cheaper.* In 1970 it cost $6.00 to get high on heroin and street level heroin was 1½ percent pure. By 1999 it cost $1.87 and street level heroin was 38 percent pure.

(3) *Drug use has increased.* There were four million people in the U.S. who had used an illegal drug in 1965 but by 2002 there were 110 million.

(4) *Corruption of public officials has increased.* Corruption of law enforcers has never been so perverse and extensive, not even under alcohol prohibition. The 500 billion dollars spent around the world on illegal drugs is not just enough to bribe a cop, a judge, or a politician, it is literally enough to buy whole countries.

(5) *The war on drugs has become a self-perpetuating policy.* In the last twenty years we have quadrupled both the number of drug arrest and the number of people sentenced to prison for those arrests. We do everything we can to destroy the hope for any future productive lives they might have then wonder why they don't stop using drugs.

Teen Drug Use Has Increased

Statistics from the 2002 study, "Monitoring the Future," which is the largest government funded study on the behaviors, attitudes, and values of American school students, indicated that from 1991 to 2002, marijuana use among students in all school grades across the country increased. How much did it increase?—30 percent of twelfth graders; 65 percent for tenths graders; and for eighth graders an 88 percent increase!

A 2002 drug survey by the National Center on Addiction And Substance Abuse at Columbia University revealed that schoolchildren across the country say it is easier for them to buy marijuana than it is to buy beer and cigarettes. The reason: When they buy those legitimate commodities, they are carded; someone wants to know how old they are. The drug dealers on the street corners or in their classrooms don't care abut their age. Show them the money and you get the drugs.

Failed Public Policy

Despite having spent over a trillion tax dollars to make more than 37 million nonviolent drug arrests while prosecuting this war; today illicit drugs are cheaper, more potent and far easier for our children to access than they were 36 years ago when I first started buying heroin as an undercover officer. That is the very definition of a failed policy.

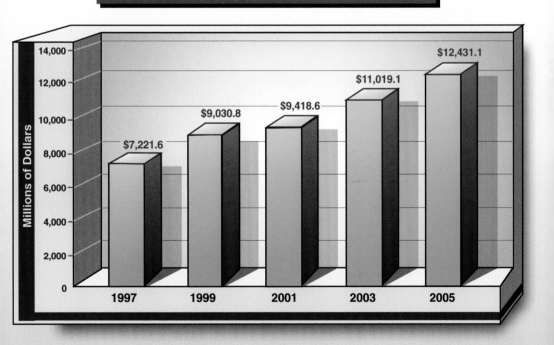

Annual Budget for the War on Drugs

Source: Office of Drug Control Policy (ONDCP).

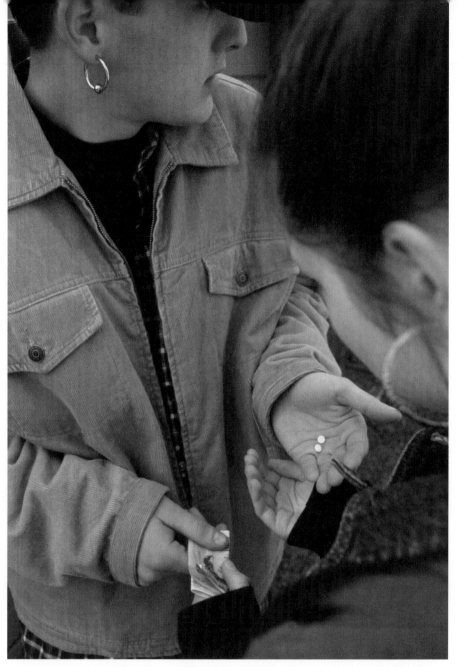

Some studies indicate that drug use among teens has risen in the last several years.

The Solution

Ending drug prohibition, just as we ended alcohol prohibition, would also end nearly all violent crime. The day alcohol prohibition ended Al Capone and all his smuggling buddies were out of business. The same thing would happen to today's drug dealers and terrorists. If drugs were legally regulated they wouldn't make a penny from drug sales.

Switzerland started a program in 1994 where they treat heroin use as a health problem. They set up clinics where users are allowed to inject free government heroin, up to three times a day. The outcomes: (1) there hasn't been an overdose death there in twelve years; (2) AIDS and Hepatitis have dropped to the lowest rates in all of Europe; (3) crime was cut by 60 percent. No one is selling heroin where these programs exist because you can't beat free. That means the dealers are not out there killing each other, cops, or kids caught in crossfire. More important, they are not in the neighborhoods enticing young novices to start using that terrible drug.

Over a ten-year period, Zurich has realized an 82 percent decline in the expected cases of new heroin users. That is a tremendous success story and one we could duplicate if we legalized and regulated all drugs. And if we treated drug abuse as a health problem instead of a crime problem we could actually save most of those young lives we are destroying through arrests and imprisonment.

EVALUATING THE AUTHORS' ARGUMENTS:

The author of this veiwpoint, Jack Cole, and the author of the previous viewpoint, Jonathan V. Last, hold very different opinions about the war on drugs. Outline their different positions and explain which author you agree with, and why.

Legalizing Drugs Would Increase Drug Abuse

U.S. Drug Enforcement Agency

"It's clear from history that periods of lax controls are accompanied by more drug abuse."

The U.S. Drug Enforcement Administration (DEA) is responsible for enforcing federal drug laws. In this viewpoint the DEA argues that history and the experience of other countries indicate that drug legalization will result in heightened drug abuse. For instance, the DEA says, morphine, opium, and cocaine addiction were widespread in the 1800s before the establishment of laws outlawing their use. Afterward, when many drugs became illegal, drug addiction levels declined dramatically. The DEA contends that the compassionate thing to do is to control and prohibit drugs until drug abuse and addiction can be eliminated.

AS YOU READ, CONSIDER THE FOLLOWING QUESTIONS:

1. What was the first broad antidrug law in the United States?
2. How many states had decriminalized marijuana by 1979?
3. What was Switzerland's experiment with drug legalization, as reported by the author?

U.S. Drug Enforcement Agency, "Speaking Out Against Drug Legalization," March 2003, pp. 14–15. www.dea.gov.

Legalization proponents claim, absurdly, that making illegal drugs legal would not cause more of these substances to be consumed, nor would addiction increase. They claim that many people can use drugs in moderation and that many would choose not to use drugs, just as many abstain from alcohol and tobacco now. Yet how much misery can already be attributed to alcoholism and smoking? Is the answer to just add more misery and addiction?

History Lessons: Opium and Cocaine

It's clear from history that periods of lax controls are accompanied by *more* drug abuse and the periods of tight controls are accompanied by less drug abuse.

During the 19th Century, morphine was legally refined from opium and hailed as a miracle drug. Many soldiers on both sides of the Civil

A nineteenth-century illustration depicts addicts smoking opium in an opium den.

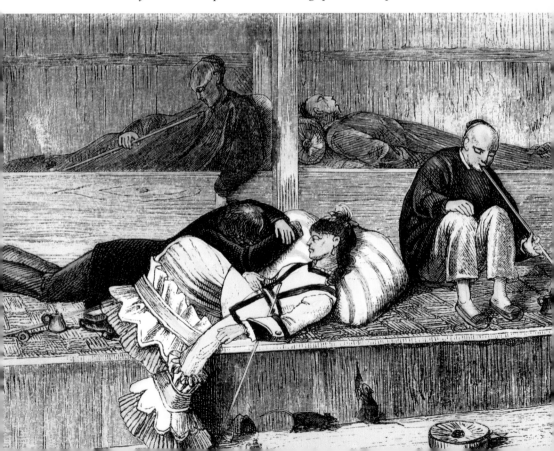

War who were given morphine for their wounds became addicted to it, and this increased level of addiction continued throughout the nineteenth century and into the twentieth. In 1880, many drugs, including opium and cocaine, were legal—and, like some drugs today, seen as benign medicine not requiring a doctor's care and oversight. Addiction skyrocketed. There were over 400,000 opium addicts in the U.S. That is twice as many per capita as there are today.

By 1900, about one American in 200 was either a cocaine or opium addict. Among the reforms of this era was the Federal Pure Food and Drug Act of 1906, which required manufacturers of patent medicines to reveal the contents of the drugs they sold. In this way, Americans learned which of their medicines contained heavy doses of cocaine and opiates—drugs they had now learned to avoid.

FAST FACT

According to Karen P. Tandy of the U.S. Drug Enforcement Agency (DEA), after marijuana use became legal in the Netherlands, consumption of marijuana nearly tripled among eigtheen- to twenty-year-olds.

Specific federal drug legislation and oversight began with the 1914 Harrison Act, the first broad anti-drug law in the United States. Enforcement of this law contributed to a significant decline in narcotic addiction in the United States. Addiction in the United States eventually fell to its lowest level during World War II, when the number of addicts is estimated to have been somewhere between 20,000 and 40,000. Many addicts, faced with disappearing supplies, were forced to give up their drug habits.

What was virtually a drug-free society in the war years remained much the same way in the years that followed. In the mid-1950s, the Federal Bureau of Narcotics estimated the total number of addicts nationwide at somewhere between 50,000 to 60,000. The former chief medical examiner of New York City, Dr. Milton Halpern, said in 1970 that the number of New Yorkers who died from drug addiction in 1950 was 17. By comparison, in 1999, the New York City medical examiner reported 729 deaths involving drug abuse. . . .

The consequences of legalization became evident when the Alaska

Some argue that legalizing drugs such as marijuana would increase drug use among teens.

Supreme Court ruled in 1975 that the state could not interfere with an adult's possession of marijuana for personal consumption in the home. The court's ruling became a green light for marijuana use. Although the ruling was limited to persons 19 and over, teens were among those increasingly using marijuana. According to a 1988 University of Alaska study, the state's 12 to 17-year-olds used marijuana at more than twice the national average for their age group. Alaska's residents voted in 1990 to recriminalize possession of marijuana, demonstrating their belief that increased use was too high a price to pay.

By 1979, after 11 states decriminalized marijuana and the Carter administration had considered federal decriminalization, marijuana

High School Seniors' Drug and Alcohol Use

Drugs Used	Last 12 Months	Last 30 Days
Alcohol	70.6%	48.0%
Marijuana	34.3%	19.9%
Stimulants	10.0%	4.6%
Other opiates	9.5%	4.3%
Tranquilizers	7.3%	3.1%
Sedatives	6.5%	2.9%
Hallucinogens	6.2%	1.9%
Cocaine	5.3%	2.3%
Inhalants	4.2%	1.5%
Steroids	2.5%	1.6%
Heroin	0.9%	0.5%

Source: Press release: Overall teen drug use continues gradual decline; but use of inhalants rises, University of Michigan News and Information Services, December 21, 2004.

use shot up among teenagers. That year, almost 51 percent of 12th graders reported they used marijuana in the last 12 months. By 1992, with tougher laws and increased attention to the risks of drug abuse, that figure had been reduced to 22 percent, *a 57 percent decline.*

Countries with Liberal Drug Laws Have Seen an Increase in Abuse

Other countries have also had this experience. The Netherlands has had its own troubles with increased use of cannabis products. From 1984 to 1996, the Dutch liberalized the use of cannabis. Surveys reveal that lifetime prevalence of cannabis in Holland increased consistently and sharply. For the age group 18–20, the increase is from 15 percent in 1984 to 44 percent in 1996.

The Netherlands is not alone. Switzerland, with some of the most liberal drug policies in Europe, experimented with what became known as Needle Park. Needle Park became the Mecca for drug addicts throughout Europe, an area where addicts could come to openly purchase drugs and inject heroin without police intervention or control. The rapid decline in the neighborhood surrounding Needle Park, with increased crime and violence, led authorities to finally close Needle Park in 1992.

The British have also had their own failed experiments with liberalizing drug laws. England's experience shows that use and addiction increase with "harm reduction" policy. Great Britain allowed doctors to prescribe heroin to addicts, resulting in an explosion of heroin use, and by the mid-1980s, known addiction rates were increasing by about 30 percent a year.

Tobacco and Alcohol Show That Legalization Leads to Increased Use

The relationship between legalization and increased use becomes evident by considering two current "legal drugs," tobacco and alcohol. The number of users of these "legal drugs" is far greater than the number of users of illegal drugs. The numbers were explored by the *2001 National Household Survey on Drug Abuse.* Roughly 109 million Americans used alcohol at least once a month. About 66 million Americans used tobacco at the same rate. But less than 16 million Americans used illegal drugs at least once a month.

It's clear that there is a relationship between legalization and increasing drug use, and that legalization would result in an unacceptably high number of drug-addicted Americans.

When legalizers suggest that easy access to drugs *won't* contribute to greater levels of addiction, they aren't being candid. The question isn't whether legalization will increase addiction levels—it will—it's whether we care or not. The compassionate response is to do everything possible to prevent the destruction of addiction, not make it easier.

EVALUATING THE AUTHORS' ARGUMENTS:

The DEA uses historical evidence and comparisons to support its claim that drug abuse will increase if drugs are made legal. Do you think analyzing events from history or the experiences of others can prove useful to make a point? Do you think the DEA's argument is persuasive?

Legalizing Drugs Would Reduce Drug Abuse

Norm Stamper

"It's time to accept drug use as a right of adult Americans."

In the following viewpoint Norm Stamper argues that drug use should not be considered criminal. Adults should be able to use any drug, including marijuana, cocaine, and heroin, as long as they do so responsibly. He suggests that those who abuse drugs or become addicted should be treated, not incarcerated. He contends that legalizing drugs could fix problems of prison overcrowding and street violence, and reduce support for terrorist groups and unstable governments. Stamper concludes that drug use should be treated as a health problem and not a criminal one.

Stamper is the former chief of the Seattle police department. He is also the author of *Breaking Rank: A Top Cop's Exposé of the Dark Side of American Policing.*

AS YOU READ, CONSIDER THE FOLLOWING QUESTIONS:

1. What is the difference between drug decriminalization and drug legalization, as described by Stamper?

2. According to Stamper, the huge increases in prison populations in the 1980s and 1990s was due to what?
3. What affect would drug legalization have on police and law enforcement personnel, according to the author?

I favor legalization, and not just of pot but of all drugs, including heroin, cocaine, meth, psychotropics, mushrooms and LSD.

Decriminalization, as my colleagues in the drug reform movement hasten to inform me, takes the crime out of using drugs but continues to classify possession and use as a public offense, punishable by fines.

I've never understood why adults shouldn't enjoy the same right to use *verboten* drugs as they have to suck on a Marlboro or knock back a scotch and water.

Prohibition of alcohol fell flat on its face. The prohibition of other drugs rests on an equally wobbly foundation. Not until we choose to

Some favor the legalization of all drugs, including cocaine (pictured).

frame responsible drug use—not an oxymoron in my dictionary—as a civil liberty will we be able to recognize the abuse of drugs, including alcohol, for what it is: a medical, not a criminal, matter. . . .

U.S. Drug Laws Are Responsible for Culture of Crime

It's not a stretch to conclude that our draconian approach to drug use is the most injurious domestic policy since slavery. Want to cut back on prison overcrowding and save a bundle on the construction of new facilities? Open the doors, let the nonviolent drug offenders go. The huge increases in federal and state prison populations during the 1980s and '90s (from 139 per 100,000 residents in 1980 to 482 per 100,000 in 2003) were mainly for drug convictions. In 1980, 580,900 Americans were arrested on drug charges. By 2003, that figure had ballooned to 1,678,200. We're making more arrests for drug offenses than for murder, manslaughter, forcible rape and aggravated assault combined. Feel safer?

I've witnessed the devastating effects of open-air drug markets in residential neighborhoods: children recruited as runners, mules and lookouts; drug dealers and innocent citizens shot dead in firefights between rival traffickers bent on protecting or expanding their markets; dedicated narcotics officers tortured and killed in the line of duty; prisons filled with nonviolent drug offenders; and drug-related foreign policies that foster political instability, wreak health and environmental disasters, and make life even tougher for indigenous subsistence farmers in places such as Latin America and Afghanistan. All because we like our drugs—and can't have them without breaking the law.

> **FAST FACT**
>
> A study funded by the U.S. National Institute on Drug Abuse and the Dutch Addiction Program found that marijuana users in San Francisco were more likely to have used cocaine, crack, amphetamines, and other drugs than were marijuana users in Amsterdam, where marijuana is legal.

As an illicit commodity, drugs cost and generate extravagant sums of (laundered, untaxed) money, a powerful magnet for character-challenged police officers.

Although small in numbers of offenders, there isn't a major police

Some theorize that legalizing drugs would reduce crime and result in a decrease in prison overcrowding.

force—the Los Angeles Police Department included—that has escaped the problem: cops, sworn to uphold the law, seizing and converting drugs to their own use, planting dope on suspects, robbing and extorting pushers, taking up dealing themselves, intimidating or murdering witnesses. . . .

Regulated Legalization
As a nation, we're long overdue for a soul-searching, coldly analytical look at both the "drug scene" and the drug war. Such candor would reveal the futility of our current policies, exposing the embarrassingly meager return on our massive enforcement investment (about $69 billion a year, according to Jack Cole, founder and executive director of Law Enforcement Against Prohibition).

How would "regulated legalization" work? It would:

1. Permit private companies to compete for licenses to cultivate, harvest, manufacture, package and peddle drugs.

Ed Hoffman, son of political activist Abbie Hoffman, hands out marijuana-related literature and paraphernalia during a legalization rally in New York City in 1996.

2. Create a new federal regulatory agency (with no apologies to libertarians or paleo-conservatives).

3. Set and enforce standards of sanitation, potency and purity.

4. Ban advertising.

5. Impose (with congressional approval) taxes, fees and fines to be used for drug-abuse prevention and treatment and to cover the costs of administering the new regulatory agency.

6. Police the industry much as alcoholic beverage control agencies keep a watch on bars and liquor stores at the state level. Such reforms would in no way excuse drug users who commit crimes: driving while impaired, providing drugs to minors, stealing an iPod or a Lexus, assaulting one's spouse, abusing one's child. The message is simple. Get loaded, commit a crime, do the time.

These reforms would yield major reductions in a host of predatory street crimes, a disproportionate number of which are committed by users who resort to stealing in order to support their habit or addiction.

Regulated legalization would soon dry up most stockpiles of currently illicit drugs—substances of uneven, often questionable quality (including "bunk," i.e., fakes such as oregano, gypsum, baking powder or even poisons passed off as the genuine article). It would extract from today's drug dealing the obscene profits that attract the needy and the greedy and fuel armed violence. And it would put most of those certifiably frightening crystal meth labs out of business once and for all.

Combined with treatment, education and other public health programs for drug abusers, regulated legalization would make your city or town an infinitely healthier place to live and raise a family.

It would make being a cop a much safer occupation, and it would lead to greater police accountability and improved morale and job satisfaction.

But wouldn't regulated legalization lead to more users and, more to the point, drug abusers? Probably, though no one knows for sure— our leaders are too timid even to broach the subject in polite circles, much leas to experiment with new policy models. My own prediction? We'd see modest increases in use, negligible increases in abuse.

Adult Americans Will Always Want to Use Drugs

The demand for illicit drugs is as strong as the nation's thirst for bootleg booze during Prohibition. It's a demand that simply will not dwindle or dry up. Whether to find God, heighten sexual arousal, relieve physical pain, drown one's sorrows or simply feel good, people throughout the millenniums have turned to mood- and mind-altering substances.

They're not about to stop, no matter what their government says or does. It's time to accept drug use as a right of adult Americans, treat drug abuse as a public health problem and end the madness of an unwinnable war.

EVALUATING THE AUTHORS'
ARGUMENTS:

Explain Stamper's idea of "regulated legalization." Do you think this idea could work? Why or why not? Use evidence from the text to support your answer.

Student Drug Testing Reduces Drug Abuse

Calvina L. Fay

"Student drug testing is one of the best ways to identify a problem . . . and get help before it is too late."

Calvina L. Fay is the executive director of the Drug Free America Foundation, a drug-prevention organization. In the following viewpoint Fay contends that drug testing is an effective tool for preventing and identifying drug problems. According to Fay, drug tests are accurate and inexpensive and help keep students who participate in extracurricular activities drug free. In addition, drug testing helps identify students who are using drugs so they can get treatment. She suggests that drug testing is so beneficial that it should be expanded to all students to keep schools drug free.

AS YOU READ, CONSIDER THE FOLLOWING QUESTIONS:
1. According to the author, what are the goals of student drug-testing programs?
2. Name two criticisms or misconceptions that the author says are commonly leveled against student drug testing.
3. What does the author mean when she says that drug testing gives students an "out"?

In his 2004 State of the Union address, President Bush not only endorsed student drug testing, but he asked for $23 million in additional government funds to implement such programs nationwide. For those in the drug abuse prevention field, this decision was paradigmatic, a firm description of what should be. Although some feel student drug testing is invasive, there is no denying it is an effective tool for identifying and preventing drug problems.

The intent of such programs is not to punish students. The goals are to deter drug use and for the drug user to straighten out his or her life. The results are not turned over to law enforcement; rather, they are discussed with the parents of the child in question so, as a family, they can discuss which type of drug treatment is suitable for their child. Drug use affects cognitive abilities and attention span, making it difficult for the user to properly learn and succeed in school. The benefits of student drug testing in addressing this abound.

U.S. president George W. Bush favors student drug testing and has asked Congress to increase funding in support of such programs.

Testing Ensures Drug-Free Student Leaders

School drug testing, as implemented today, applies only to students who voluntarily choose to participate in athletic and extracurricular activities. Student athletes and students in extracurricular activities take leadership roles in the school community and, as role models, should be drug-free—and student drug testing helps ensure this. More importantly, it gives students in extracurricular activities an "out" or an argument that they can use with drug-using peers when pressured to take drugs (e.g., "If I take drugs, the coach will know because I have to take a drug test, and then I'll be kicked off the team"). Today, drug testing is a standard procedure when applying for a job. Certainly, athletes who want to compete at the collegiate or Olympic level should get used to the idea of drug testing.

Drug Testing Is Accurate

Some people criticize drug testing on grounds it can be inaccurate. This charge is incorrect. The drug-testing procedures in place today eliminate the possibility of a false positive. If schools follow drug-testing procedures recommended by the White House Office of National Drug Control Policy, students will provide a urine specimen in a private rest-room area. The specimen will be handled under the chain of custody guidelines, a set of procedures to account for the integrity of each urine specimen by tracking its handling and storage from collection to disposition of the specimen. If the screening test is positive, confirmation is sought with a more sensitive test. If the confirmation test is positive, a physician trained in drug testing then reviews it and contacts the student to see if there is a legitimate medical reason for the positive result. Drug test results are confidential, and federal law prevents them from being released outside the school. And the results do not follow the student once he or she leaves high school (as per the Family Educational Rights and Privacy Act).

Most Commonly Tested Substances

A 2004 study surveyed school districts that engage in student drug testing. Marijuana, methamphetamine, and opiates ranked among the most commonly tested-for substances.

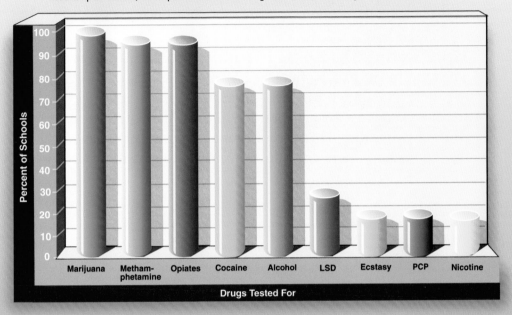

Source: Western Illinois University, "Student Random Drug Testing Survey," February 2004.

Drug Testing Is Worth the Small Cost

Another misconception about student drug testing is that it is expensive and difficult to implement. A drug test costs only between $10 and 30 per student, a cost that is nominal compared to its true worth. Any school that receives federal education funding is permitted to use these funds for drug testing; the No Child Left Behind Act specifically authorizes the expenditure of federal education funds for student drug testing. So, if the money is there, let's put it to good use.

I have worked with many like-minded individuals on this issue who all agree that student drug testing is a deterrent, although effective only when coupled with other drug-prevention and -education initiatives. Along these lines, attorney David Evans is making many important strides with the Drug-Free Schools Coalition in New Jersey. Evans stresses an important point when he says, "Many schools find great value in using random drug and alcohol testing [for student athletes and those in extracurricular activities] as part of their antidrug programs. The goal of drug testing is to deter drug and alcohol use. Students who know they may be detected are less likely to use drugs or alcohol, not to mention experience the consequences of addiction."

Drug Testing Should Be Expanded to All Students

The unfortunate part of student drug testing today is that we cannot test those who do not participate in extracurricular activities. These students encounter the same peer pressure that the extracurricular students face, but they don't have the same drug-testing defense, making it potentially more difficult to say no to drugs. Although schools

Many proponents of drug testing in schools believe the entire student population must be tested.

that test athletes and students in other extracurricular activities experience an overall decline in drug use, they must not forget about those students who do not benefit from drug testing and at least provide them with other drug-prevention and -education alternatives.

As a drug-policy and -prevention expert with more than 20 years' experience, I have fought for this issue alongside many parents who have lost their children to drugs. These parents have told me time and time again, "I never suspected that my child was using drugs. If I had only known, I could have done something." It kills me every time I hear this. Student drug testing is one of the best ways to identify a problem and offer a chance for parents to know about it and get help before it is too late.

EVALUATING THE AUTHORS' ARGUMENTS:

Fay writes that all students should be drug tested. If you were in charge of the schools in your community, would you test students for drugs? If so, which students or group of students would you test? What drugs would you test for? Explain your answers.

Viewpoint 6

Student Drug Testing Does Not Reduce Drug Abuse

Nikos A. Leverenz

"Drug testing has a poor track record in reducing student drug use."

In the following viewpoint Nikos A. Leverenz argues against student drug testing. He claims that no scientific evidence shows that drug testing prevents or reduces student drug abuse. Even if such evidence existed, he contends, student drug testing should not be used because it is expensive and infringes on students' rights to privacy. According to Leverenz, there are more effective ways to combat adolescent drug abuse.

Leverenz is an analyst at the Drug Policy Alliance, an organization that seeks to change drug laws and policy in the United States.

AS YOU READ, CONSIDER THE FOLLOWING QUESTIONS:
1. What does the word "hyperbole" mean in the context of the viewpoint?
2. What does the author suggest helps combat substance abuse issues?
3. According to Leverenz, why do politicians and bureaucrats support drug-testing programs?

Nikos A. Leverenz, "Testing the Wrong Policy on Students," *Brainwash*, September 19, 2004. Reproduced by permission.

The evidence thus far is clear: drug testing has a poor track record in reducing student drug use, particularly in comparison to other drug prevention and education programs. Its fiscal toll on local school budgets saps money that would be better spent on basic educational needs. Drug testing also undermines parental authority, as parents have no input as to whether their child will be tested. Most ominously, the practice creates future citizens who become accustomed to ever-broader government surveillance as merely routine.

Despite these concerns, the federal government is using a wide array of public resources—monetary and institutional—to advance drug testing in schools nationwide. In 2002, the Office of National Drug

Urine samples are placed in a centrifuge to be tested for illegal substances. Whether drug testing reduces teen drug use is not clear cut.

Control Policy (ONDCP) issued a booklet called "What You Need to Know About Drug Testing in Schools." The stated goal of the booklet is to "shed light and offer perspective on this multifaceted and sometimes controversial topic.". . .

Student Drug Testing Is Ineffective

Drug Czar John Walters touts drug testing as a "silver bullet" to combat student drug use. The best available scientific evidence shows otherwise. For example, a study of 960 schools with 94,000 students conducted by scientists who the federal government relies on for its Monitoring the Future survey of adolescent substance use, concluded: [Drug testing] is found not to be associated with students' reported illicit drug use—even random testing that potentially subjects the entire student body. Testing was not found to have significant association with the prevalence of drug use among the entire student body nor the prevalence of use among experienced marijuana users.

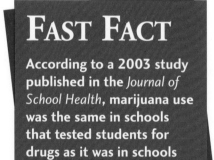

FAST FACT

According to a 2003 study published in the *Journal of School Health*, marijuana use was the same in schools that tested students for drugs as it was in schools that did not test for drugs.

The American Academy of Pediatrics has also weighed in on drug testing programs targeting student-athletes and others involved in "competitive extracurricular activities." Its Committee on Substance Abuse issued a formal policy statement that rejected the use of drug testing to combat substance abuse: "Voluntary screening" is the term applied to many mass non-suspicion-based screening programs, yet such programs may not be truly voluntary as there are often negative consequences for those who choose not to take part. Participation in such programs should not be a prerequisite to participation in school activities.

This position stands in stark contrast to the increasingly widespread practice of schools requiring students to submit to drug testing as a condition of participation in extracurricular activities. Drug testing programs that deter or deprive students from participation in such activities are entirely counterproductive. Participation in such activities is the most effective method of combating the prob-

Some believe mandatory drug testing deters teens from participating in sports, which in turn makes them more susceptible to experimenting with drugs.

lems of substance use, pregnancy, and crime among juveniles.

Drug testing is a medical tool that is intended for two primary purposes: to support the diagnosis of substance abuse and addiction, and to facilitate treatment of those recovering from substance abuse and addiction. Medical practitioners do not consider testing a 'silver bullet' in either case, however. As the American Medical Association notes: "Drug testing does not provide any information about pattern of use of drugs, abuse of or dependence on drugs, or about mental or physical impairments that may result from drug use."

The opinions of the scientific and medical communities aside, Walters also deliberately downplays individual privacy implications. In a

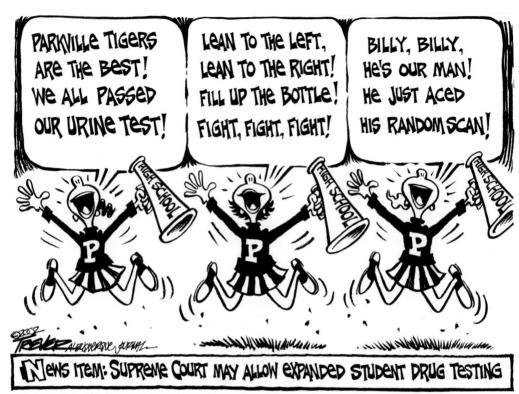

John Trevor. Reproduced by permission of Cagle Cartoons, Inc.

2003 *Education Week* interview he said, "I don't think the privacy arguments pertain in the case of this disease [addiction]. . . . I'm not talking about reading kids' diaries." His foreword to the ONDCP booklet states that privacy concerns are "unfounded" and that those who focus on them "ignore the enormous potential benefits of drug testing."

[Former] Attorney General John Ashcroft . . . shares the ONDCP's callous disregard of individual rights on the drug-testing front. His Department of Justice offers legal counsel to school districts facing court challenges to their drug testing programs.

The Justice Department compounds its erroneous approach to adolescent drug policy by its continued financial support of the Drug Abuse Resistance Education (D.A.R.E.) program. D.A.R.E., like student drug testing, has not been proven to deter adolescent drug and alcohol use. Because of its dubious effectiveness, the Department of Education's Safe and Drug-Free Schools Program has withheld grant money since 1998.

Supporters of Student Drug Testing Are Misguided

Politicians and bureaucrats support programs like D.A.R.E. and student drug testing because they address an important social problem—adolescent substance use—without taking big risks to really solve the problem. As with other misguided government "crusades," failure actually substantiates the call for more resources devoted to ephemeral outcomes like "enormous potential benefits." The high costs of such meaningless hyperbole are buttressed by the pervasive political desire to use police officers and schoolchildren as human props on the grand stage of government.

Thus the federal government's ongoing commitment to a costly, ineffective policy boondoggle like student drug testing is unsurprising. What is more notable is Washington's quiet yet powerful bureaucratic assault on this nation's parents and students. Individual liberties—and those constitutional values acknowledging them—should not be blithely regarded as pesky inconveniences by those who are charged with their protection.

EVALUATING THE AUTHORS' ARGUMENTS:

In the viewpoint you just read, Leverenz argues that drug testing infringes on students' privacy. In the previous viewpoint Fay argues that although some regard testing as invasive, it effectively prevents drug abuse. In your opinion, is drug testing an invasion of students' privacy? If not, why not? If so, is it worth it?

Chapter 3

What Role Does Marijuana Play in Drug Abuse?

The legalization of marijuana has been a subject of controversy for decades.

Marijuana Is Harmful

U.S. Office of Drug Control Policy

"Marijuana use can lead to increased anxiety, panic attacks, depression, and other mental health problems."

In the following viewpoint the Office of Drug Control Policy (ONDCP) says that marijuana's damaging effects are especially harmful to young people. Marijuana impairs brain activity when teenage brains are still developing. As a result, kids who smoke marijuana have difficulty learning and are often depressed and anxious. Moreover, kids will keep using marijuana even when it interferes with school or family relationships, illustrating the drug's powerful pull and addictive nature.

The ONDCP is the main drug-fighting organization in the United States. It was established by the federal government in 1988 to oversee the nation's antidrug efforts and advise the president on drug control policies.

AS YOU READ, CONSIDER THE FOLLOWING QUESTIONS:
1. Why, according to the ONDCP, is marijuana use particularly harmful for kids?
2. List four drugs that disrupt the flow of chemical neurotransmitters in the brain.
3. What is the DSM and what does it contain, according to the viewpoint?

U.S. Office of Drug Control Policy, *Marijuana: Myths & Facts, The Truth Behind 10 Popular Misconceptions*, pp. 3–8. www.whitehousedrugpolicy.gov/publications/marijuana_myths_facts.

Marijuana harms in many ways, and kids are the most vulnerable to its damaging effects. Use of the drug can lead to significant health, safety, social, and learning or behavioral problems, especially for young users. Making matters worse is the fact that the marijuana available today is more potent than ever.

Short-term effects of marijuana use include memory loss, distorted perception, trouble with thinking and problem-solving, and anxiety. Students who use marijuana may find it hard to learn, thus jeopardizing their ability to achieve their full potential.

Cognitive Impairment

That marijuana can cause problems with concentration and thinking has been shown in research funded by the National Institute on Drug

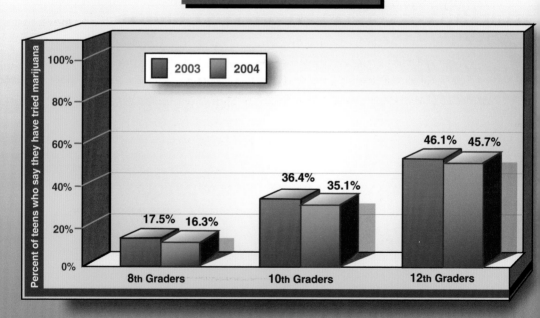

Teen Marijuana Use

Source: National Institute on Drug Abuse and University of Michigan, Monitoring the Future 2004. Data from in-school surveys of 8th-, 10th-, and 12th- grade students, December 2004.

Abuse (NIDA), the federal agency that brings the power of science to bear on drug abuse and addiction. A NIDA-funded study at McLean Hospital in Belmont, Massachusetts, is part of the growing body of research documenting cognitive impairment among heavy marijuana users. The study found that college students who used marijuana regularly had impaired skills related to attention, memory, and learning 24 hours after they last used the drug.

Another study, conducted at the University of Iowa College of Medicine, found that people who used marijuana frequently (7 or more times weekly for an extended period) showed deficits in mathematical skills and verbal expression, as well as selective impairments in memory-retrieval processes. These findings clearly have significant implications for young people, since reductions in cognitive function can lead to poor performance in school.

FAST FACT

According to the DEA, each year more teens enter drug treatment programs with a primary diagnosis of marijuana dependence than for all other illicit drugs combined.

Other impairments observed in frequent marijuana users involve sensory and time perception and coordinated movement, suggesting use of the drug can adversely affect driving and sports performance. Effects such as these may be especially problematic during teens' peak learning years, when their brains are still developing.

Mental Health Problems

Smoking marijuana leads to changes in the brain similar to those caused by cocaine, heroin, and alcohol. All of these drugs disrupt the flow of chemical neurotransmitters, and all have specific receptor sites in the brain that have been linked to feelings of pleasure and, over time, addiction. Cannabinoid receptors are affected by THC, the active ingredient in marijuana, and many of these sites are found in the parts of the brain that influence pleasure, memory, thought, concentration, sensory and time perception, and coordinated movement.

Particularly for young people, marijuana use can lead to increased anxiety, panic attacks, depression, and other mental health problems. One study linked social withdrawal, anxiety, depression, attention problems, and thoughts of suicide in adolescents with past-year marijuana use. Other research shows that kids age 12 to 17 who smoke marijuana weekly are three times more likely than non-users to have thoughts about committing suicide. A recently published study showed that use of cannabis [i.e., marijuana] increased the risk of major de-

Studies show that teens who use marijuana can experience depression and anxiety.

Marijuana use can impair a person's ability to drive safely.

pression fourfold, and researchers in Sweden found a link between marijuana use and an increased risk of developing schizophrenia.

Traffic Safety

Marijuana also harms when it contributes to auto crashes or other incidents that injure or kill, a problem that is especially prevalent among young people. In a study reported by the National Highway Traffic Safety Administration, even a moderate dose of marijuana was shown to impair driving performance. The study measured reaction time and how often drivers checked the rear-view mirror, side streets, and the relative speed of other vehicles.

Another study looked at data concerning shock-trauma patients who had been involved in traffic crashes. The researchers found that 15 percent of the trauma patients who were injured while driving a car or motorcycle had been smoking marijuana, and another 17 percent had both THC and alcohol in their blood. Statistics such as these are particularly troubling in light of recent survey results indicating that almost 36 million people age 12 or older drove under the influence of alcohol, marijuana, or another illicit drug in the past year.

Longterm Consequences

The consequences of marijuana use can last long after the drug's effects have worn off. Studies show that early use of marijuana is strongly associated with later use of other illicit drugs and with a greater risk of illicit drug dependence or abuse. In fact, an analysis of data from the National Household Survey on Drug Abuse showed that the age of initiation for marijuana use was the most important predictor of later need for drug treatment.

EVALUATING THE AUTHORS' ARGUMENTS:

The author of this viewpoint, the ONDCP, is a government agency and the viewpoint is supported by statistics and research studies from other governmental agencies. Does this enhance the persuasiveness or validity of the arguments? Why?

Marijuana Is Not Harmful

Paul Armentano

"Almost all drugs— including those that are legal— pose greater threats to individual health and/or society than does marijuana."

In this viewpoint Paul Armentano refutes assertions made by the Office of National Drug Control Policy (ONDCP) that marijuana is harmful. Saying that the ONDCP and other policy makers are lying to the public about marijuana, Armentano points to scientific studies which conclude that marijuana is relatively safe when compared to other drugs. Armentano says that marijuana cannot cause death by overdose, and cites studies that show it does not cause cancer and is not addictive. Furthermore, Armentano says alcohol and tobacco, two legal drugs, are much more harmful and addictive than marijuana.

Armentano is a senior policy analyst with NORML, a nonprofit lobbying organization that seeks to legalize marijuana.

AS YOU READ, CONSIDER THE FOLLOWING QUESTIONS:

1. According to Armentano, what damage is caused by overstating marijuana's potential harms?
2. What effect does marijuana have on the brain, according to the author?
3. According to the U.S. Institute of Medicine, what percentage of marijuana users exhibit symptoms of dependence?

Paul Armentano, "Your Government Is Lying to You (Again) About Marijuana: An Updated Refutation of the Drug Czar's "Open Letter to America's Prosecutors"," *The 2005 NORML Truth Report*, July 21, 2005. Reproduced by permission.

Since [2002], the White House's anti-marijuana propaganda campaign has continued to take on an increasingly alarmist and extremist tone, arguably crossing over any reasonable line of probity. The Bush Administration's latest rhetoric does not qualify as mere exaggeration; they are flat-out lying to the American public about marijuana.

As a result, NORML has updated and greatly expanded our 2003 report [entitled, "Your Government Is Lying to You (Again) About Marijuana"]. Like our initial paper, the "2005 NORML Truth Report" relies on the federal government's own science, data, and statistics to rebut the Drug Czar's lies and propaganda. . . .

Let's allow science, not rhetoric, to dictate America's public policy regarding marijuana. As you will see, the facts speak for themselves. . . .

Marijuana Is Less Dangerous than Other Drugs

[Some officials have said] "Nationwide, no drugs matches the threat posed by marijuana."

A devastating car crash serves as a reminder of how dangerous driving under the influence of alcohol can be. Some marijuana advocates argue that it is safer than alcohol.

This statement is pure hyperbole. *By overstating marijuana's potential harms, America's policy-makers and law enforcement community undermine their credibility and ability to effectively educate the public of the legitimate harms associated with more dangerous drugs like heroin, crack cocaine, and methamphetamine.*

In fact, almost all drugs—including those that are legal—pose greater threats to individual health and/or society than does marijuana. According to the Centers for Disease Control, approximately 46,000 people die each year from alcohol-induced deaths (not including motor vehicle fatalities where alcohol impairment was a contributing factor), such as overdose and cirrhosis. Similarly, more than 440,000 premature deaths annually are attributed to tobacco smoking. By comparison, marijuana is non-toxic and cannot cause death by overdose. . . .

After an exhaustive, federally commissioned study by the National Academy of Sciences' Institute of Medicine (IOM) in 1999 examining all of marijuana's potential health risks, authors concluded, *"Except for the harms associated with smoking, the adverse effects of marijuana use are within the range tolerated for other medications."* . . . The IOM further added, *"There is no conclusive evidence that marijuana causes cancer in humans, including cancers usually related to tobacco use."* . . .

> ## FAST FACT
>
> A *Journal of Neuroscience* study showed that cannabinoids, chemicals that are naturally found in marijuana, can reduce inflammation in the brain and may protect it from the cognitive decline associated with Alzheimer's disease.

Numerous studies and federally commissioned reports have endorsed marijuana's relative safety compared to other drugs, and recommended its decriminalization or legalization. Virtually all of these studies have concluded that *the criminal "classification of cannabis is disproportionate in relation both to its inherent harmfulness, and to the harmfulness of other substances."* Even a pair of editorials by the premiere British medical journal, *The Lancet*, acknowledge: "The smoking of cannabis, even long-term, is not harmful to health. . . . It would be reasonable to judge cannabis as less of a threat . . . than alcohol tobacco." . . .

Lies About Marijuana's Effects on the Brain

Allegations that marijuana smoking alters brain function or has long-term effects on cognition are reckless and scientifically unfounded. Federally sponsored population studies conducted in Jamaica, Greece and Costa Rica found no significant differences in brain function between long-term smokers and non-users. Similarly, a 1999 study of 1,300 volunteers published in *The American Journal of Epidemiology* reported *"no significant differences in cognitive decline between heavy users, light users, and nonusers of cannabis"* over a 15-year period. More recently, a meta-analysis of neuropsychological studies of long-term marijuana smokers by the National Institute on Drug Abuse reaf-

Some studies indicate that marijuana does not have long-term, negative effects on the brain.

Advocates of marijuana argue that alcohol is a more addictive drug.

firmed this conclusion. In addition, a study published in the *Canadian Medical Association Journal* in April 2002 reported that even former heavy marijuana smokers experience no negative measurable effects on intelligence quotient.

Most recently, researchers at Harvard Medical School performed magnetic resonance imaging on the brains of 22 long-term cannabis users (reporting a mean of 20,100 lifetime episodes of smoking) and 26 controls (subjects with no history of cannabis use). Imaging displayed "no significant differences" between heavy cannabis smokers compared to controls. "These findings are consistent with recent literature suggesting that cannabis use is not associated with structural changes within the brain as a whole or the hippocampus in particular," authors concluded. . . .

Marijuana Is Not Addictive

Marijuana use is not marijuana abuse. According to the US Institute of Medicine's 1999 Report: "Marijuana and Medicine: Assessing the Science Base," "Millions of Americans have tried marijuana, but most are not regular users, . . . [and] few marijuana users become dependent on it." In fact, *less than 10 percent of marijuana users ever exhibit symptoms of dependence* (as defined by the American Psychiatric Association's DSM-IV criteria). By comparison 15 percent of alcohol users, 17 percent of cocaine users, and a whopping 32 percent of cigarette smokers statistically exhibit symptoms of drug dependence.

Marijuana is well recognized as lacking the so-called "dependence liability" of other substances. According to the IOM, "Experimental animals that are given the opportunity to self administer cannabinoids generally do not choose to do so, which has led to the conclusion that they are not reinforcing or rewarding." Among humans, most marijuana users voluntarily cease their marijuana smoking by their late 20s or early 30s—often citing health or professional concerns and/or the decision to start a family. Contrast this pattern with that of the typical tobacco smoker—many of whom begin as teens and continue smoking daily the rest of their lives.

EVALUATING THE AUTHORS' ARGUMENTS:

The author of this viewpoint and the author of the opposing viewpoint both contend that science is on their side. They each point to scientific studies and in some cases even use the same study to back their claims. How do you account for this? After reading both viewpoints, what do you think—is marijuana harmful or not?

Marijuana Leads to Abuse of Other Drugs

National Center on Substance Abuse and Addiction at Columbia University

"Most users of other illicit drugs have used marijuana first."

The National Center for Substance Abuse and Addiction at Columbia University (CASA) focuses on combating and reducing drug abuse in the United States. The organization, which was formed in 1992, conducts research and publishes reports on various substance abuse issues. In this viewpoint CASA contends that research studies and statistics abound to support the argument that marijuana is a "gateway" drug, meaning that it leads to the use of other drugs. According to CASA, the more often and earlier a child uses marijuana, the likelier that child is to use harder drugs such as cocaine, methamphetamines, or heroin. On the other hand, CASA suggests that a child who reaches adulthood without smoking marijuana will probably never use other drugs.

AS YOU READ, CONSIDER THE FOLLOWING QUESTIONS:

1. In addition to marijuana, what other drugs does this viewpoint say are gateways to illicit drug use?

"Non-Medical Marijuana II: Rite of Passage or Russian Roulette?," *The National Center on Substance Abuse and Addiction at Columbia University*, April, 2004, p. 15–16. Reproduced by permission.

According to the viewpoint, a teen who has used marijuana is how many times more likely to use other drugs such as cocaine or heroin than a teen who has never used marijuana?

3. What did the twin study find, as reported by CASA? What is the significance of using same-sex twins?

The association between the use of marijuana and other drugs is well established: most current cocaine and heroin users have already used marijuana, and people who use marijuana are at higher risk for using other illegal drugs. The Institute of Medicine's 1999 report, *Marijuana and Medicine: Assessing the Science Base*, states: "Not surprisingly, most users of other illicit drugs have used marijuana first. In fact, most drug users begin with alcohol and nicotine before marijuana—usually before they are of legal age. In the sense that marijuana use typically precedes rather than follows initiation of other illicit drug use, it is indeed a 'gateway' drug. But because underage smoking and alcohol use typically precede marijuana use, marijuana is not the most common, and is rarely the first, 'gateway' to illicit drug use."

FAST FACT

According to a study reported in the *Journal of the American Medical Association*, a study of three hundred sets of twins revealed that marijuana-using twins were four times more likely than their nonusing siblings to use cocaine and five times more likely to use LSD.

Statistics Link Marijuana to Hard Drugs

CASA [Center on Substance Abuse and Addiction] established a statistical relationship between current use of marijuana—in and of itself—and the use of harder drugs such as cocaine, heroin, methamphetamines, LSD and Ecstasy. For this study, CASA conducted a special analysis of data from the 2001 U.S. Centers for Disease Control and Prevention Youth Risk Behavior Survey of 11,000 ninth through twelfth graders, and isolated teen use of these gateway drugs from other problem behaviors such as fighting, drunk driving, carrying a weapon and attempting suicide. The conclusion: among teens

One of the concerns about marijuana use is that it may lead to the abuse of harder drugs such as heroin (pictured).

aged 12 to 17 with no other problem behaviors, those who used marijuana at least once in the past 30 days are 13 times likelier than those teens who have not used marijuana in the past 30 days (33.5 percent vs. 4.4 percent) to use another drug like cocaine, heroin, methamphetamines, LSD or Ecstasy, and almost 26 times likelier than those

A curious girl observes her friends prepare to smoke marijuana.

teens who have never used marijuana (33.5 percent vs. 1.3 percent) to use another drug like cocaine, heroin, methamphetamines, LSD or Ecstasy. To appreciate the significance of this relationship, consider this: the first U.S. Surgeon General's report on cigarette smoking and health in 1964 found a nine to 10 times greater risk of lung cancer among cigarette smokers, and the early results of the extensive Framingham heart study [50 years of data collected from the residents of Framingham, MA] found that individuals with high cholesterol were two to four times likelier to suffer heart disease.

Study of Twins: Marijuana Might Cause Other Drug Use

Some have argued that the association between marijuana and other drugs may be explained by drug use propensity—that is, that marijuana and other drug initiation are correlated because both are influenced by individuals' unique propensities to try drugs—rather than by a causal or "gateway" effect. However, a recent study of 311 same-sex twin pairs from Australia found that early marijuana use by itself significantly increased the likelihood of other drug use, even after controlling for genetic and environmental influences. Individuals who used marijuana by age 17 were up to 3.9 times likelier to use other drugs and up to 6 times likelier to experience alcohol dependence and other drug abuse/dependence, relative to their twin who had not used marijuana by age 17. By controlling for environmental and genetic factors, this study is a compelling indicator that the use of marijuana in and of itself is predictive of, and may even cause, the later use of other illicit drugs.

For parents of teens and those teachers, clergy and coaches who work with teens, the message is clear: marijuana use is not only dangerous in and of itself, it is an alarm that signals a higher risk of other drug use.

EVALUATING THE AUTHORS' ARGUMENTS:

CASA contends that there is enough scientific evidence to show that marijuana use leads to the use of other drugs. Based on the studies and statistics presented in this viewpoint, were you persuaded? Why or why not? Explain your answer.

Marijuana Use Does Not Lead to Abuse of Other Drugs

Common Sense for Drug Policy

"The research indicates most marijuana users do not go on to use hard drugs."

Common Sense for Drug Policy is a non-profit organization that works to reform drug policy in the United States. In this viewpoint the organization argues that most kids who use marijuana do not go on to use other drugs. They say that although it is true that most people who use hard drugs probably did use marijuana first, this fact proves nothing. Marijuana is more prevalent and accessible, and more likely to be tried first. Marijuana use is irrelevant to drug users' decisions to move on to hard drugs. The organization says that if everyone who tried marijuana went on to use hard drugs, millions more people would have used cocaine and heroin than do now.

AS YOU READ, CONSIDER THE FOLLOWING QUESTIONS:
1. According to the federal government, how many people have tried marijuana? How many people have tried heroin?

Common Sense for Drug Policy, "Distortion 7: Gateway Theory," Drug War Distortions, October 20, 2005. www.drugwardistortions.org.

2. What was the control group that was used in the study published in the *Journal of the American Medical Association*?
3. According to the viewpoint, what two drugs are better than marijuana at predicting later use of hard drugs?

T he 'gateway' claim is a myth. Marijuana is the most widely used illicit drug so it is very likely that people who use less commonly-used drugs will have also tried marijuana. That does not mean marijuana led to hard drug use. The research indicates

The claim that marijuana is a "gateway" to the abuse of harder drugs is strongly debated.

most marijuana users do not go on to use hard drugs; marijuana is more properly viewed as a strainer that catches most illicit drug users and they go no further. The numbers bear out these findings: According to the federal government 76.3 million people have tried marijuana, while only 2.78 million have ever tried heroin in their lifetimes and only 5.3 million have ever tried cocaine in their lives. The figures for monthly use are similar: 10.7 million Americans admit to being regular marijuana users, yet only 1.2 million admit to using cocaine each month—1 for every 9 marijuana users—and 130,000 people use heroin monthly, or 1 for every *80* regular marijuana users. . . .

Twin Study Shows Marijuana Associated with Later Drug Use but Not Causing It

The Journal of the American Medical Association features an article on 'gateway theory' in its Jan. 22/29, 2003 edition. According to the article, "Early Onset of Drugs Use in Early-Onset Cannabis [i.e., marijuana] Users vs. Co-twin Controls," "While the findings of this study

Jars of marijuana line a coffee shop counter in Amsterdam, Netherlands, where the drug is legal.

indicate that early cannabis use is associated with increased risks of progression to other illicit drug use and drug abuse/dependence, it is not possible to draw strong causal conclusions solely on the basis of the associations shown in this study."

Indeed, according to the study's authors:

"Other mechanisms that might mediate a causal association between early cannabis use and subsequent drug use and drug abuse/dependence include the following:

Initial experiences with cannabis, which are frequently rated as pleasurable, may encourage continued use of cannabis and also broader experimentation.

Seemingly safe early experiences with cannabis may reduce the perceived risk of, and therefore barriers to, the use of other drugs. For example, as the vast majority of those who use cannabis do not experience any legal consequences of their use, such use may act to diminish the strength of legal sanctions against the use of all drugs.

Alternatively, experience with and subsequent access to cannabis use may provide individuals with access to other drugs as they come into contact with drug dealers. This argument provided a strong impetus for the Netherlands to effectively decriminalize cannabis use in an attempt to separate cannabis from the hard drug market. This strategy may have been partially successful as rates of cocaine use among those who have used cannabis are lower in the Netherlands than in the United States."

Tobacco and Alcohol More Gateway than Marijuana

Indeed, rather than cannabis, the research seems to point to early use of tobacco or alcohol as more of a predictor of later use of other drugs and of later problem drug use. The report notes that . . . early regular use of tobacco and alcohol emerged as the 2 factors most consistently associated with later illicit drug use and abuse/dependence. . . .

> **FAST FACT**
>
> According to the United Nations Office on Drugs and Crime, in 2005 close to 160 million people in the world used marijuana, but only 11 million used heroin and about 14 million people used cocaine.

According to some, alcohol is more likely than marijuana to spur experimentation with different drugs.

Marijuana as Gateway Dismissed by the Institute of Medicine

The Institute of Medicine in 1999 dismissed the 'gateway' theory:

"There is no conclusive evidence that the drug effects of marijuana are causally linked to the subsequent abuse of other illicit drugs.". . .

The IOM report went further:

"Patterns in progression of drug use from adolescence to adulthood are strikingly regular. Because it is the most widely used illicit drug, marijuana is predictably the first illicit drug most people encounter. Not surprisingly, most users of other illicit drugs have used marijuana first. In fact, most drug users begin with alcohol and nicotine before marijuana—usually before they are of legal age."

EVALUATING THE AUTHORS' ARGUMENTS:

Both this viewpoint and the previous viewpoint say that the research supports its arguments that marijuana is or is not a gateway drug. Which viewpoint do you think uses the research more convincingly to support its argument? Why?

Drug Abuse in America

- The Office of National Drug Control Policy reports that the most commonly used illegal drugs by those over the age of twelve are:
  - marijuana: 12.1 million users, or 5.4 percent of the population
  - cocaine: 1.7 million users, or 0.7 percent of the population
  - hallucinogens (e.g., LSD, PCP, and ecstasy): 1.3 million users, or 0.6 percent of the population

According to the 2004 National Survey on Drug Use and Health:

- 110 million Americans aged twelve or over (45.8 percent of the U.S. population) report having used an illicit drug at least once.
- Approximately 36 million Americans have reported abusing prescription drugs at least once in their lifetime.
- Among the 16.7 million heavy drinkers in America, 32.2 percent are also illicit drug users.
- An estimated 10.6 million persons reported driving under the influence of an illicit drug during the past year.

Drug Abuse Treatment

- The Drug Abuse Warning Network (DAWN) estimated that in 2004 there were more emergency room visits in the United States involving the abuse of prescription drugs (495,732 visits) than for cocaine (383,350 visits), marijuana (215,665 visits), or heroin (162,137 visits).
- According to the U.S. Centers for Disease Control, injection-drug use has directly and indirectly accounted for more than one-third (36 percent) of AIDS cases in the United States since the epidemic began.

According to the 2004 National Survey on Drug Use and Health:

- An estimated 3.8 million people aged twelve or older (1.6 percent of the population) received some kind of treatment for a problem related to the use of alcohol or illicit drugs in 2004.
- Of these, 1.5 million received treatment for the use of both alco-

hol and illicit drugs, and 0.7 million received treatment for the use of illicit drugs but not alcohol.

- In 2004 males were more than twice as likely as females to receive treatment for an alcohol or an illicit drug use problem in the past year.

The U.S. Substance Abuse and Mental Health Services Administration reports:

- Five substances accounted for about 95 percent of all substance abuse treatment admissions in 2004:
  - alcohol (40 percent)
  - opiates, primarily heroin (18 percent)
  - marijuana (16 percent)
  - cocaine (14 percent)
  - stimulants, primarily methamphetamine (8 percent)

Drug Abuse in Schools

According to the 2005 University of Michigan *Monitoring the Future* survey:

- Over 80 percent of students say that they would disapprove of trying an inhalant.
- Annual use of LSD among twelfth graders has been below 10 percent since the study began in 1975.
- The proportion of twelfth graders saying that it would be "fairly easy" or "very easy" for them to get cocaine if they wanted to was 45 percent in 2005.
- The proportion of twelfth-grade students saying they could get heroin fairly easily if they wanted to was 30 percent.
- Annual rates for methamphetamine use in 2005 were down considerably from the first measurement taken in 1999. In 1999, 3.2 percent of eighth graders, 4.6 percent of tenth graders, and 4.7 percent of twelfth graders reported using methamphetamines. In 2005, just 1.8 percent of eighth graders, 2.9 percent of tenth graders, and 2.5 percent of twelfth graders reported using methamphetamines.
- More school-aged boys than girls report steroid use. In 2005 annual rates of steroid use were 1.2 percent, 1.8 percent, and 2.6 percent for boys in grades 8, 10, and 12, compared with 0.9 percent, 0.7 percent, and 0.4 percent for girls.

Facts About the Costs of Drug Abuse

- President Bush asked the U.S. Congress for almost $19.6 million to spend on student drug testing in schools for fiscal year 2007.
- In 2005 the U.S. government spent approximately $12.6 billion to fight drug use and abuse, including about $2 billion for stopping drug use, about $3 billion for healing drug users, and about $7.5 billion to disrupt drug supply markets.
- In 2002 the total cost of drug abuse to the United States was estimated at $180.9 billion per year.

The War on Drugs

- According to the U.S. Bureau of Justice Statistics, more than half (55 percent) of federal prisoners are serving time for a drug offense.
- According to the Sentencing Project, women in prison are more likely than men (32 percent vs. 21 percent) to be serving a sentence for a drug charge.
- According to the Federal Bureau of Investigation's Uniform Crime Report, in 2004, 39 percent of all drug abuse violations were for marijuana possession.

Facts About Marijuana

- According to the U.S. Drug Enforcement Agency, average levels of THC (the main active ingredient) in marijuana have risen from less than 1 percent in the mid-1970s to more than 8 percent in 2004.
- A 50 percent concentration of THC can be found in the body—particularly the testes, liver, and brain—up to eight days after using marijuana. Traces of THC can be found in the body up to three months after use.
- As of June 2006 eleven states have medical marijuana laws that make it permissible for people with certain debilitating diseases to grow or possess marijuana.
- According to the National Survey on Drug Use and Health, students with an average grade of "D" or below were four times as likely to have used marijuana in the past year as students who reported an average grade of "A."
- The U.S. Substance Abuse and Mental Health Services Adminis-

tration reports that three-quarters of primary marijuana substance-abuse treatment admissions were male.

The National Institute on Drug Abuse reports:

- Marijuana is the most commonly used illegal drug in the United States.
- Nearly 45 percent of U.S. teenagers try marijuana before finishing high school.

American Civil Liberties Union (ACLU)
125 Broad St., 18th Floor
New York, NY 10004-2400
(212) 549-2500
e-mail: aclu@aclu.org
Web site: www.aclu.org

The ACLU is a national organization that works to defend Americans' civil rights guaranteed by the U.S. Constitution. It provides legal defense, research, and education. The ACLU opposes the criminal prohibition of marijuana and the civil liberties violations that result from it.

American Council for Drug Education (ACDE)
164 W. 74th St.
New York, NY 10023
(800) 488-DRUG
e-mail: acde@phoenixhouse.org
Web site: www.acde.org

The American Council for Drug Education informs the public about the harmful effects of abusing drugs and alcohol. It gives the public access to scientifically based, compelling prevention programs and materials.

Cato Institute
1000 Massachusetts Ave. NW
Washington, DC 20001-5403
(202) 842-0200
e-mail: service@cato.org
Web site: www.cato.org

The institute is a public policy research foundation dedicated to limiting the control of government and to protecting individual liberty. Cato, which strongly favors drug legalization, publishes the *Cato Journal* three times a year and the *Cato Policy Report* bimonthly.

Drug Enforcement Administration (DEA)
2401 Jefferson Davis Hwy.
Alexandria, VA 22301
(202) 307-1000
Web site: www.dea.gov

The DEA is the federal agency charged with enforcing the nation's drug laws. The agency concentrates on stopping the smuggling and distribution of narcotics in the United States and abroad. It publishes the *Drug Enforcement Magazine* three times a year.

The Drug Policy Alliance
70 W. 36th St., 16th Floor
New York, NY 10018
(212) 613-8020
e-mail: dc@drugpolicy.org
Web site: www.dpf.org/homepage.cfm

The Drug Policy Alliance is the leading organization in the United States promoting alternatives to the war on drugs. The Alliance supports the creation of drug policies that respect individual rights, protect community health, and minimize the involvement of the criminal justice system.

The Drug Reform Coordination Network
1623 Connecticut Ave. NW, 3rd Floor
Washington, DC 20009
(202) 293-8340
e-mail: drcnet@drcnet.org
Web site: http://stopthedrugwar.org

The Drug Reform Coordination Network opposes the war on drugs and works for drug-policy reform from a variety of perspectives, including harm reduction, reform of sentencing and forfeiture laws, medicalization of marijuana, and the promotion of an open debate on drug prohibition.

Join Together
One Appleton St., 4th Floor
Boston, MA 02116-5223
(617) 437-1500
e-mail: info@jointogether.org
Web site: www.jointogether.org

Founded in 1991, Join Together supports community-based efforts to reduce, prevent, and treat substance abuse. It publishes community action kits to facilitate grassroots efforts to increase awareness of substance abuse issues as well as a quarterly newsletter.

Marijuana Policy Project
PO Box 77492-Capitol Hill
Washington, DC 20013
(202) 462-5747
e-mail: mpp@mpp.org
Web site: www.mpp.org

The Marijuana Policy Project develops and promotes policies to minimize the harm associated with marijuana. It is the only organization that is solely concerned with lobbying to reform the marijuana laws on the federal level.

Multidisciplinary Association for Psychedelic Studies (MAPS)
10424 Love Creek Rd.
Ben Lemond, CA 95005
(831) 336-4325
e-mail: askmaps@maps.org
Web site: www.maps.org

MAPS is a membership-based research and educational organization. It focuses on the development of beneficial, socially sanctioned uses of psychedelic drugs and marijuana. MAPS helps scientific researchers obtain governmental approval for funding of psychedelic research on human volunteers.

National Center on Addiction and Substance Abuse at Columbia University (CASA)
633 Third Ave., 19th Floor
New York, NY 10017-6706
(212) 841-5200
Web site: www.casacolumbia.org

CASA is a private nonprofit organization that works to educate the public about the costs and hazards of substance abuse and the prevention and treatment of all forms of chemical dependency. The center supports treatment as the best way to reduce drug addiction.

National Clearinghouse for Alcohol and Drug Information
PO Box 2345
Rockville, MD 20847-2345
(800) 729-6686
e-mail: shs@health.org
Web site: www.health.org

The clearinghouse distributes publications of the U.S. Department of Health and Human Services, the National Institute on Drug Abuse, and other federal agencies concerned with alcohol and drug abuse. Brochure titles include *Tips for Teens About Marijuana.*

National Institute on Drug Abuse (NIDA)
6001 Executive Blvd., Room 5213 MSC 9561
Bethesda, MD 20892-9561
(301) 443-6245
e-mail: information@nida.nih.gov
Web site: www.nida.nih.gov

NIDA supports and conducts research on drug abuse—including the yearly *Monitoring the Future* survey—to improve addiction prevention, treatment, and policy efforts. It publishes the bimonthly *NIDA Notes* newsletter, periodic "NIDA Capsules," fact sheets, and a catalog of research reports and public education materials, such as *Marijuana: Facts for Teens* and *Marijuana: Facts Parents Need to Know.*

National Organization for the Reform of Marijuana Laws (NORML)
1600 K St. NW
Washington, DC 20006
(202) 483-5500
e-mail: norml@norml.org
Web site: www.norml.org

NORML fights to legalize marijuana and to help those who have been convicted and sentenced for possessing or selling marijuana. In addition to pamphlets and position papers, it publishes the newsletter *Marijuana Highpoints,* the bimonthly *Legislative Bulletin* and *Freedom@NORML,* and the monthly *Potpourri.*

Office of National Drug Control Policy (ONDCP)
PO Box 6000
Rockville, MD 20849-6000
(800) 666-3332
e-mail: ondcp@ncjrs.org
Web site: www.whitehousedrugpolicy.gov

The Office of National Drug Control Policy is responsible for formulating the government's national drug strategy and the president's antidrug policy as well as coordinating the federal agencies responsible for stopping drug trafficking. Drug policy studies are available upon request.

Partnership for a Drug-Free America
405 Lexington Ave., Suite 1601
New York, NY 10174
(212) 922-1560
Web site: www.drugfreeamerica.org

The Partnership for a Drug-Free America is a nonprofit organization that utilizes media communication to reduce demand for illicit drugs in America. Best known for its national antidrug advertising campaign, the partnership works to "unsell" drugs to children and to prevent drug use among kids.

Books

Fish, Jefferson M., ed., *Drugs and Society: U.S. Public Policy.* Lanham, MD: Rowman & Littlefield, 2006. This book presents several chapters each devoted to different aspects of drugs, their impact on society, and the public policies that control them.

Fitzhugh, Karla, *Prescription Drug Abuse.* Chicago, IL: Heinemann Library, 2006. From a series of books called *What's the Deal?* this title looks at prescription drug abuse and the pros and cons of particular choices young people must make about their behavior.

Goode, Erich, *Drugs in American Society.* 6th ed. New York: McGraw-Hill, 2004. Provides a balanced and up-to-date investigation of drug use in all of its social, cultural, and legal complexity.

Huggins, Laura E., ed., *Drug War Deadlock: The Policy Battle Continues.* Stanford, CA: Hoover Institution, 2005. Presents a diverse collection of readings from scholarly journals, government reports, think tank studies, newspapers, and books that offer a comprehensive look at the drug debate.

Inciardi, James A., and Karen McElrath, eds., *The American Drug Scene: An Anthology.* 4th ed. Los Angeles: Roxbury, 2004. A collection of contemporary and classic articles on legal and illegal drugs including opiates, cocaine, marijuana, hallucinogens, alcohol, and tobacco. Topics include gender and addiction, sexual identity and drug use, the symbolic meaning of drug taking, HIV/AIDS as it relates to injection-drug use, and the relationship between drugs and violence.

Kelley, Margaret S., ed., *Readings on Drugs and Society: The Criminal Connection.* Boston: Pearson Allyn and Bacon, 2006. The author brings together leading contemporary research on the relationship between drugs and crime, with a focus on street crime.

Kuhn, Cynthia, Scott Swartzwelder, Wilkie Wilson, Leigh Heather Wilson, and Jeremy Foster, *Buzzed: The Straight Facts About the Most Used and Abused Drugs from Alcohol to Ecstasy.* 2nd. ed. New York: W.W.

Norton, October 2003. This guide presents unbiased, straightforward scientific information in an easy-to-read style about drugs such as marijuana, alcohol, caffeine, ecstacy, hallucinogens, herbal drugs, inhalants, and many others.

Masters, Bill, ed., *The New Prohibition: Voices of Dissent Challenge the Drug War*. Lonedell, MO: Accurate Press, May 2004. Features twenty-one essays that challenge the core assumptions of the war on drugs.

Rebman, Renee, *Addictions and Risky Behaviors: Cutting, Bingeing, Snorting, and Other Dangers*. Berkeley Heights, NJ: Enslow, 2006. This teen-focused book presents the dangers and addiction potential of many risky behaviors, including alcohol, inhalants, and smoking.

Rees, Jonathan, *Drugs*. North Mankato, MN: Smart Apple Media, 2006. Raises important questions about drug abuse, such as why people take drugs and if drugs should be legalized.

Rowe, Thomas C., *Federal Narcotics Laws and the War on Drugs: Money Down a Rat Hole*. Binghamton, NY: Haworth, 2006. Examines the current antidrug programs and policies in the United States, explains why they have failed, and presents a plan to fix them.

Singer, Merrill, *Something Dangerous: Emergent and Changing Illicit Drug Use and Community Health*. Long Grove, IL: Waveland, 2005. Discusses the changing underground world of drug use and its associated health effects.

Sullum, Jacob, *Saying YES: In Defense of Drug Use*. New York: Tarcher, 2003. Sullum asserts that all drugs, including heroin, cocaine, and marijuana, can be used responsibly. Presents real life stories of responsible drug users who are not the stereotypical addicts.

Wexler, Bob, and Linda Wexler, *Losing Johnathon*. New Bedford, MA: Spinner, 2003. Tells the heart-wrenching story of Bob and Linda Wexler's son Johnathon, who was addicted to heroin and died of a drug overdose.

Periodicals

Amodio, Joseph V., "How Marijuana Messes with Your Brain and Body," *Current Health 2*, March 1, 2005.

Brinkley, Joel, "U.S. Lists Its Pluses and Minuses in Fighting Narcotics Worldwide," *New York Times*, March 2, 2006.

Caulkins, Jonathon P., Peter Reuter, Martin Y. Iguchi, and James Chiesa,

"How Goes the 'War on Drugs'? An Assessment of U.S. Drug Problems and Policy," Rand Drug Policy Research Center, 2005.

Childress, Sarah, "My Mother the Narc: Do Home Drug-Testing Kits Help or Hurt Teens?" *Newsweek*, April 10, 2006.

Creech, Mark H., "Prohibition and the Legalization of Drugs," *Agape Press*, November 22, 2005.

Cronkite, Walter, "Telling the Truth About the War on Drugs," *Huffington Post*, March 1, 2006. www.huffingtonpost.com.

Curley, Bob, "Treatment No Panacea for Nation's Drug Problems," *Join Together Online*, April 28, 2006. www.jointogether.org.

Ebenkamp, Becky, "Sex, Drugs & R'n'R High School. National Survey of American Attitudes on Substance Abuse X: Teens and Parents." *Brandweek*, September 5, 2005.

Economist, "Just Say Maybe: Illegal Drugs," April 5, 2003.

Flaherty, Mary Pat, "Study Cites Drug Abuse 'Epidemic' Among Teens," *Washington Post*, July 7, 2005.

Friedman, R.A., "The Changing Face of Teenage Drug Abuse—The Trend Toward Prescription Drugs," *New England Journal of Medicine*, April 6, 2006.

Gottlieb, Scott, "A Legion of Little Helpers. We're All Performance-Enhancers Now. Hypocrites, Too," *Wall Street Journal*, December 10, 2004.

Hertzberg, Hendrik, "Watched Pot," *New Yorker*, June 27, 2005.

Hoag, Hannah, "Seeing the Big Picture. Creation of a Drug," *Nature*, April 20, 2006.

Kern, Jennifer, Fatema Gunja, Alexandra Cox, Marsha Rosenbaum, Judith Appel, and Anjuli Verma, "Making Sense of Student Drug Testing: Why Educators Are Saying No," *Drug Policy Alliance*, January 2006. www.drugtestingfails.org.

Kleiman, Mark A.R., "Flying Blind on Drug Control Policy," *Issues in Science and Technology Online*, Summer 2004. www.issues.org.

Leinwand, Donna, "Drugmakers Take Action to Foil Meth Cooks," *USA Today*, June 29, 2005.

Lewinsohn, Jed, "A Third Way on Drug Law," *American Enterprise*, September 2003.

Males, Mike, "What Do Student Drug Use Surveys Really Mean?" *Journal of School Health*, January 2005.

McVay, Doug, Vincent Schiraldi, and Jason Ziedenberg, "Treatment or Incarceration: National and State Findings on the Efficacy of Drug Treatment Versus Imprisonment," Justice Policy Institute, March 2004. www.justicepolicy.org.

Miller, Sara B., "Steps Toward More Drug Testing in Schools," *Christian Science Monitor*, May 20, 2005.

Muir, Hazel, "An Epidemic of Home-Made Hits: Tampering with Prescription Drugs Is on the Rise, and the Internet Is Making It Easier than Ever," *New Scientist*, June 3, 2006.

Nadelmann, Ethan, "An End to Marijuana Prohibition: The Drive to Legalize Picks Up," *National Review*, 2004.

National Institute on Drug Abuse Research Report Series: Prescription Drugs Abuse and Addiction, rev. August 2005. www.nida.nih.gov/researchreports.

Querna, Elizabeth, "Pot Head," *US News & World Report*, February 8, 2005.

Ribeiro, Michele Lee, and Sarah Richards, "When Prescription Drugs Kill," *CosmoGirl!* March 7, 2005.

Satel, Sally, "Much Ado About Meth?" *TCS Daily*, November 4, 2005.

Saturday Evening Post Junior Edition, "'Pharming' a Danger to Teens," May/June 2006.

Science World, "Prescription Drugs: Their Use and Abuse," March 6, 2006.

Walters, John P., "No Surrender: The Drug War Saves Lives," *National Review*, September 27, 2004.

Will, George, "This War Is Worth Fighting," *Washington Post*, June 16, 2005.

Web Sites

Drug Watch International (www.drugwatch.org). Drug Watch International is a nonprofit drug information and advocacy organization that promotes the creation of healthy drug-free cultures in the world and opposes the legalization of drugs.

Harm Reduction Journal (www.harmreduction.com). *Harm Reduc-*

tion Journal is an online journal that focuses on finding effective ways to reduce the adverse medical and social consequences associated with drug abuse.

Just Think Twice (www.justthinktwice.com). Just Think Twice is a teen-focused Web site sponsored by the U.S. Drug Enforcement Administration to raise public awareness about the dangers of drugs. It is designed to present facts straightforwardly in a way that can help teens make smart choices about drug use.

Justice Policy Institute (www.justicepolicy.org). The Justice Policy Institute is a nonprofit research and public policy organization dedicated to ending society's reliance on incarceration and promoting effective and just solutions to drug abuse and other social problems.

Index

crimes related to, 27–29, 67
drug availability and, 54
federal agency statistics about,
    48–49
as health problem throughout
    human history, 71
Internet and, 43
legalization and, 56, 58–60,
    65–71
legalization of marijuana and, 67
methamphetamine use and crime,
    28–29
19th century history of, 60–61
overdose statistics, 25
potency of drugs and, 54
prisons and, 18, 19
prohibition and, 56–57
reality of, 71
statistics about Americans and,
    17–18
substances abused in America, 39
War on Drugs and, 47–51,
    52–57
see also marijuana; student drug
    testing; teen drug abuse
Drug Abuse Resistance Education
    program (DARE), 16, 82, 83
Drug Czar. *See* Walters, John
Drug Free America Foundation, 72
Drug-Free Schools Coalition,
    75–76
Drug Policy Alliance, 78
Drug Watch International, 9
DSM-IV criteria, 96
Dutch marijuana legalization
    program, 60, 63, 67, 105

Ecstasy ("X"), 16, 98, 99
Equipoise, 41
Evans, David, 75–76

Family Educational Rights and
    Privacy Act, 74
Fay, Calvina L., 72–77

FDA (Food and Drug
    Administration), 43
Federal Bureau of Narcotics, 60
Federal Pure Food and Drug Act of
    1906, 60
Ferrer, Miguel, 48
Food and Drug Administration
    (FDA), 43

Halpern, Milton, 60
"harm reduction" model, 23–24
Harrison Act, 60
Harvard Medical School, 95
heroin, 16, 98, 99, 105
HHS (U.S. Department of Health
    and Human Services), 48–49

inhalants, 16
Institute of Medicine (IOM), 93,
    96, 98, 106–7
International Task Force on
    Strategic Drug Policy, 11
Internet, 43

"Journal of School Health," 80
*Journal of the American Medical
    Association* (JAMA), 98
"Just Say No" campaign, 49
Justice Department, 82–83

Lancet (medical journal), 93
Last, Jonathan V., 47–51
Law Enforcement Against
    Prohibition (LEAP), 52, 53–54,
    68
legalization of drugs
    alcohol policy and, 63
    argument against, 58–64
    arguments for, 56–57, 65–71
    regulated program for, 68, 70–71
    tobacco policy and, 63
    see also marijuana
Leverenz, Nikos A., 78–83
LSD, 51, 98, 99

Males, Mike, 20–25
Maran, Meredith, 14–19
marijuana
    addiction and, 90
    Alaska experience with, 52, 60
    arguments against legalizing,
        85–90
    brain changes and, 87–89, 94–95
    compared with tobacco, 96
    decriminalization result, 63
    as "gateway" drug, 97–101
    as harmful, 85–90
    as leading to other drug abuse,
        90, 97–101
    as less dangerous than other
        drugs, 92–93
    mental health problems caused
        by, 87–89
    negative consequences of using,
        90
    Netherlands' legalization program
        for, 60, 63, 67, 105
    as predictor of addiction, 90
    statistics linking to hard drug use,
        98–99
    statistics proving link to drug
        abuse, 98–100
    studies of, 98, 100–101
    teenagers and, 16
    traffic safety and, 89–90
"Marijuana and Medicine: Assessing
    the Science Base," 96, 98
Marlett, Alan, 10
meth labs, 27, 31
methamphetamine (meth) abuse
    child abuse and, 30–31
    children and, 27, 29–31
    cold medicine crackdown and, 37
    compared with alcohol or
        cigarettes, 34, 36
    crime and, 27
    effects of, 29
    as epidemic, 26–31
    as exaggeration, 32–37

impact of, 31
marijuana and, 98, 99
pregnancy during, 29–30
production of, 27
sources of, 26
statistics about student use of, 34
toxic waste and, 27
"Monitoring the Future" (national
    study of high school students),
    54–55
morphine, 59–60

National Academy of Sciences, 93
National Association of Counties
    (NACo), 26–31
National Center for Substance
    Abuse and Addiction (CASA),
    97–101
National Center on Addiction and
    Substance Abuse (CASA), 21, 22,
    38, 39, 54–55
National Highway Traffic Safety
    Administration, 89–90
National Household Survey on
    Drug Abuse, 90
National Institute on Drug Abuse
    (NIDA), 87, 94–95
National Institutes of Health
    (NIH), 48–49
Needle Park, 63
Netherlands' marijuana legalization
    program, 60, 63, 67, 105
Newsweek (magazine), 33
nicotine. See tobacco
NIDA (National Institute on Drug
    Abuse), 87, 94–95
NIH (National Institutes of
    Health), 48–49
No Child Left Behind Act, 75
NORML (nonprofit organization
    for marijuana legalization),
    91–96

Office of National Drug Control

cost of to U.S. economy, 18
as crisis in American society,
     14–19
decreases in, 21, 49
distorted statistics about, 21–22
ease of drug access and, 41,
     54–55
effects of , 87
as exaggerated, 21–22
failure of, 15–16
high school senior statistics for,
     62
increases in, 49, 54
Internet and, 43
legal drugs and, 22
marijuana use statistics and, 86
mental health problems from,
     87–89
methods used to control, 15–16
parents' role in, 44
prescription drugs and, 39–40,
     41–42
statistics about, 16
War on Drugs and, 49–50
see also drug abuse; marijuana;
     student drug testing; teenagers
teenagers
     addiction and, 21, 22–23
     drug and alcohol use, 62
     "harm reduction model" and,
          23–24
     marijuana and, 16, 25, 86
     scare tactics and, 24
     as using drugs responsibly, 23–24
     as using milder drugs, 25
     see also student drug testing; teen
          drug abuse
Terhune, Tom, 37
Time (magazine), 34
tobacco, 63, 98, 105
Traffic (movie), 48
traffic safety, 89–90
tranquilizers, 16

twin studies for marijuana research,
     98, 100–101, 104–5
*2001 National Household Survey on
     Drug Abuse*, 63

U.S. Department of Health and
     Human Services (HHS), 48–49
U.S. Institute of Medicine (IOM),
     93, 96, 98, 106–7
U.S. Drug Enforcement Agency
     (DEA), 50, 58–64

Valium, 39, 41
Vicodin, 41
"voluntary screening". *See* student
     drug testing

Walters, John, 51, 80, 81–82
War on Drugs
     argument against, 52–57
     argument for, 47–51
     cost of, 55
     organizations opposing, 52, 53,
          102
     statistics favoring, 49, 50, 51
     statistics supporting opposition
          to, 54–55
     as success, 47–51
     war on terror and, 53
Weekly Standard (magazine), 47
"What You Need to Know About
     Drug Testing in Schools"
     (booklet), 80
White House Office of National
     Drug Control Policy, 74

"X" (Ecstasy), 16, 98, 99
Xanax, 41

"Your Government Is Lying to You
     (Again) About Marijuana"
     (report), 92
Youth Today (newsletter), 20

Picture Credits

Cover: Bananastock/Jupiter Images
Altrendo/Getty Images, 22
AP Photos, 68, 69, 73
© C. Devan/zefa/CORBIS, 48
Danny Moloshok/Landov, 46
David Young-Wolff/Photo Edit, 61
Dennis MacDonald/Jupiter Images, 92
Frank Siteman/Jupiter Images, 94
Getty Images, 10, 11, 36
© H. Benser/zefa/CORBIS, 24
© Hekimian Julien/SYGMA/CORBIS, 79
Iconica/Getty Images, 40
© James Leynse/CORBIS, 15
Linda Lewis/Jupiter Images, 84
© Martin Meyer/zefa/CORBIS, 13
Maury Aaseng, 18, 28, 55, 62, 75, 86
North Wind Pictures, 59
Oliver Grove/PYMCA/Jupiter Images, 35
© Owen Franken/CORBIS, 104
Photo Researchers, Inc., 33
PhotoDisc, 100
Reuters/Landov, 50
Rex Interstock/Jupiter Images, 103
© Sandra Seckinger/zefa/CORBIS, 89
© SGO/Image Point FR/CORBIS, 44
Stone/Getty Images, 23
Taxi/Getty Images, 56, 76, 88, 99
© The Cover Story/CORBIS, 66
Time Life Pictures/Getty Images, 42
Timothy Shonnard/Jupiter Images, 106
© Tom Stewart/CORBIS, 81
Yannick Fagot/Jupiter Images, 95

Jacqueline Langwith does policy research for the Michigan Legislative Service Bureau in the areas of biotechnology, biomedicine, controlled substances, climate change, alternative energy, and the generation of electric power. She has a Masters Degree in Biochemistry from Michigan Technological University (MTU). Prior to her position at the Bureau, Ms. Langwith managed the Plant Biotechnology Research Center at MTU.

DATE DUE